| | PINE VALLEY INTERMEDIATE | | |
| | 3000 Pine Valley Road | | 76 |
| | San Ramon, CA 94583 | | |

| DATE | NAME | TEACHER | BOOK COND. |
|------|------|---------|------------|
| 9/9/99 | Rey | Hegarty | B-5 |
| 9/2/03 | Ariele Herring | Hegarty | |
| 9/5/ | | | |
| 9/1/09 | Peter Hong | Hegarty | |
| 8-30-11 | Isaac Breinyn | Hegarty | |
| | | | |
| | | | |
| | | | |
| | | | |
| | | | |

# *Nothing but the Truth*

a documentary novel

## and Related Readings

McDougal Littell
A HOUGHTON MIFFLIN COMPANY

Evanston, Illinois    *Boston*    *Dallas*

*Acknowledgments*

**Bantam Doubleday Dell Publishing Group, Inc.:** "honesty," from
*archys life of mehitabel* by Don Marquis. Copyright 1927, 1933 by
Doubleday, a division of Bantam Doubleday Dell Publishing
Group, Inc. Used by permission of Doubleday, a division of
Bantam Doubleday Dell Publishing Group, Inc.
**Harcourt Brace & Company:** "A Nice Old-Fashioned Romance, with
Love Lyrics and Everything," from *My Name Is Aram*. Copyright
1940 and renewed © 1968 by William Saroyan. Reprinted by per-
mission of Harcourt Brace & Company.
**Simon & Schuster:** Excerpt from *Journey to Washington* by Daniel
K. Inouye with Lawrence Elliot. Copyright © 1967 by Prentice
Hall, Inc. Renewed © 1995. Reprinted with the permission of
Simon & Schuster.
**National Council of Teachers of English:** "For LB, 1943–1993" by
Cecil Morris from *English Journal*, March 1995. Copyright © 1995
by the National Council of Teachers of English. Reprinted with
permission.
**Rosemary A. Thurber:** "The Catbird Seat," from *My World—And
Welcome To It* by James Thurber, published by Harcourt Brace.
Copyright 1942 James Thurber, Copyright © 1970 Rosemary A.
Thurber.

*Nothing But The Truth* by Avi; Copyright © 1991 by Avi.
Reprinted by permission of the publisher, Orchard Books, New
York. All rights reserved.

Author photo: Coppelia Kahn

ISBN 0-395-77536-1

567—DCI—02 01 00 99 98

# *Contents*

*Continued*

# Nothing but the Truth

a documentary novel

Avi

**Two Questions**
Do you swear to tell the truth
the whole truth, and
nothing but the truth?

Does anyone say no?

# MEMO

## HARRISON SCHOOL DISTRICT

### Where Our Children Are Educated, Not Just Taught

Dr. Albert Seymour 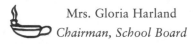 Mrs. Gloria Harland
*Superintendent* *Chairman, School Board*

## STANDARD FORMAT FOR MORNING ANNOUNCEMENTS ON PUBLIC-ADDRESS SYSTEM

1. 8:05 A.M. The Principal, or in his stead the Assistant Principal, or in his stead a designated member of the faculty, will say, "Good morning to all students, faculty, and staff. Today is Monday (or whatever day), January (or whatever month) 3 (or whatever day). Today will be a Schedule A (or B) day" (depending on what schedule).

2. Say, "Today in history . . ." (Please consult *Book of Days* in Principal's office for appropriate references. Limit is three items.)

3. Say, "Please all rise and stand at respectful, silent attention for the playing of our national anthem."

4. Turn on tape of anthem.

5. After anthem is complete, say, "I have these announcements." All administration and faculty announcements shall be made at this point.

6. Say, "May I now introduce          (name of student, grade) for today's sport and club news. Have a good day."

7. Student announcements.

8. All announcements should end by 8:15 latest.

Dr. Joseph Palleni
*Assistant Principal*

# Chapter 1

Tuesday, March 13

Coach Jamison saw me in the hall and said he wanted to make sure I'm trying out for the track team!!!! Said my middle school gym teacher told him I was really good!!!! Then he said that with me on the Harrison High team we have a real shot at being county champs. Fantastic!!!!!! He wouldn't say that unless he meant it. Have to ask folks about helping me get new shoes. Newspaper route won't do it all. But Dad was so excited when I told him what Coach said that I'm sure he'll help.

Saw a thing on TV about Olympic committees already organizing all over the country. Olympics. I'm going to be there! County champs. State champs. College champs. Then Olympics! Folks always reminding me about the money they're putting aside for my college, which is the only way to go. That's what did Dad in, dropping out. Too hard to get noticed with just clubs.

Rainy and cold. I hate this kind of weather. Slows you down. Still ran six miles. I'm getting stronger.

Oh, yeah. . . . At lunch Sarah Gloss came up and said she had to speak to me. Said this girl, Allison

Doresett, likes me. I had to act cool because I wasn't sure who she was. Then I remembered she's in my English class and is really decent. She must have liked that gag question I asked. The two of us would be front-of-the-line. Bet she heard about my running too. Girls go for guys who win. Ta-da! It's Malloy Magic time!

Talk about Malloy Magic. . . . This time for—da-dum!—Miss Narwin. I mean, what can you do with an English teacher who's so uptight she must have been put together with super glue. Try to make a joke—lighten things up a bit—she goes all flinty faced. Shift to sweet, she goes sour. I mean, people can't have their own minds about anything!!! Talk about a free country!!! And the stuff we have to read! Can't believe how stupid and *boring* Jack London is! I mean, really, *The Call of the Wild*. Talk about dogs! Ma says she had to read it when *she* was in school. There has to be better stuff to read for ninth grade somewhere. I thought high school was going to be different.

Have to figure a way to run past Narwin.

---

**10:45 P.M.**
**From a Letter Written by**
**Margaret Narwin**
**to Her Sister, Anita Wigham**

---

Yes, Anita, I suppose that after doing *anything* for twenty-one years a body does get a little tired. And I *have* been teaching English at Harrison High for just that long. All the same, I remain steadfast in my belief that my life was meant to be *the bringing of fine literature to young minds*. When the connection is made—and from time to time it *is* made—it's all worth it. Is it wrong to speak of the work as a calling? Well, teaching *is* almost a religion to me. I will complain from time to time, but—it *is* my life. The truth is, I like it.

But the *other* truth, Anita, is that students today are not what they used to be. There is no love of literature. Not the way you and I learned it from Mother. Young people don't read at all today—outside of school requirements. They come to literature reluctantly at best, fighting me every inch of the way. It's not as if they aren't bright. They *are*. And I like them and their capacity for independence. But the other side of that independence is a lack of caring for anything beyond themselves. If they ask me once more "What's this have to do with *us?*" I think I'll scream. Of course, I don't scream. You have to treat them with care *and* fairness. Fairness is *so* important to them.

For example: these days I'm teaching *The Call of the Wild*. A student raised his hand to say he didn't understand "who was calling who." Now if I were to laugh or mock, he would be insulted. And I would lose him.

This boy, Philip Malloy, is new to me. I met his parents at First Night, and they seem like pleasant folks; they come regularly to PTA meetings. They are educated—she is, anyway. I'm not sure what they do.

But this Philip—an only son, by the way, which may be the problem—is only a middling student, and it's a shame. A nice-looking boy. A boy I like. Intelligent. With real potential. Perhaps that's why he irritates me so—for he shows no desire to strive, to make sacrifices for the betterment of self, the way we were taught. And, oh, my, Anita, so restless! Worst of all, like so many of them, he exhibits *no* desire to learn. No ambition at all! But it's not even *that* I mind so much. No, it's a certain something—a resistance—to accepting the idea that literature is important. For him or anyone! But it is. *It is!* If I could only convince students of that. It's that desire that keeps me going.

I can hear you saying, "Come on down to Florida." Anita, I don't know if I am ready for that yet.

Yes, I could take early retirement. Mr. Benison (Science) is doing so. But then, he's older than I. And he has a wife who works. The truth is, Anita, I would be lost without my books, my teaching, my students.

I had a note from Ethel Truebel! Do you remember her? She used to be in the West Fork Church congregation years ago. It seems . . .

# Chapter 2

Thursday, March 15

---

**8:05 A.M.
Discussion
in Bernard Lunser's
Homeroom Class**

---

MR. LUNSER: Let's go! Let's go! *Carpe diem.* Time to grab the moment!

INTERCOM VOICE OF DR. GERTRUDE DOANE, HARRISON HIGH PRINCIPAL: Good morning to all students, faculty, and staff. Today is Thursday, March 15. Today will be a Schedule A day.

MR. LUNSER: Get that, bozos? A day!

DR. DOANE: Today in history: on this day in 44 B.C., Julius Caesar was assassinated.

MR. LUNSER: And right after that they all sat down and ate a Caesar salad.

DR. DOANE: In 1767, Andrew Jackson, our seventh president, was born.

MR. LUNSER: So by the time this here Andy's term was over, he was four years old.

DR. DOANE: It was in 1820 that Maine was admitted to the United States.

**MR. LUNSER:** And by 1821 they wanted out.

**DR. DOANE:** Please all rise and stand at respectful, silent attention for the playing of our national anthem.

*Oh, say, can you see by the dawn's early light,*
*What so proudly we hailed at the twilight's last*
*gleaming? . . .*

**MR. LUNSER:** Okay, Philip, is that yesterday's homework or today's you're working on?

*Whose broad stripes and bright stars, thro' the perilous*
*fight . . .*

**PHILIP MALLOY:** I'm trying to pass an exam.

**MR. LUNSER:** Ah, the famous wit and wisdom of Mr. Malloy. Philip, I'm the only one allowed to make jokes around here. Put the book away.

*O'er the ramparts we watched were so gallantly*
*streaming? . . .*

**PHILIP MALLOY:** Just one last paragraph?

**MR. LUNSER:** Away, Philip! Or I'll make you sing along solo!

*And the rockets' red glare, the bombs bursting in air,*
*Gave proof thro' the night that our flag was still there.*
*Oh, say does that star-spangled banner yet wave*
*O'er the land of the free and the home of the brave?*

**MR. LUNSER:** Okay. Move it out! Move it out! Hey, and be careful in those hallways.

**STUDENT:** What about announcements?

**MR. LUNSER:** Seems there aren't any, for which we can all be grateful. Anyway, Philip needs the time to study for his exam!

Winter term exams next week. Hate them. Studying is so boring! I read the biology book for about twenty minutes tonight. Then I realized I wasn't really *reading*. Must have been asleep or something.

Three exams scheduled in one day!!! The trick is getting past the teacher. It's like a race. You have to have a strategy—know when to take it easy, know when to turn on the juice. Get teachers to *think* you're in control. Have to know when to kick. Like— put in one of *their* ideas. Or when all else fails make them laugh.

The exam I really want to study for is math. I could get a good mark. People think I'm weird, but I like math.

I won't waste time on English. What can you say about a dog? Besides, it's just a matter of opinion, anyway!!! If I could only get Narwin to crack a smile.

Mom and Dad have been arguing a lot lately. Wonder what *that* means? Dad said his business is in a cash flow squeeze. Mom says the phone company wants employees to pay more into the health plan. Says that's not fair. Dad says the point of business is to make the most money.

Been checking Allison out. She looked cool today. Dad says that when you're a sports star girls really go for you. Hey, Allison, remember me? Phil. Phil Malloy. Right! How would you like a box seat at the Olympics?

Mr. Bentcroft—on Washington Street—owes me for three weeks of newspapers. Talk about dogs!!!!

Sunny at first today. Then cloudy. Bit of rain. Then sunny again. Still, I got in a couple of hours of workout. Mostly wind sprints. Then twenty minutes on Dad's rowing machine.

In *Running* magazine, there's this guy, Steve Hallick, who's 17, and he's doing the 55 meters in 6.51 seconds!!!!

Track team practice season starts next week. Can't wait. That's all Dad and I talk about.

# Chapter 3

## Friday, March 16

---

### MEMO

---

### HARRISON SCHOOL DISTRICT

Where Our Children Are Educated,
Not Just Taught

Dr. Albert Seymour<br>
*Superintendent*  Mrs. Gloria Harland<br>
*Chairman, School Board*

TO: PHILIP MALLOY
FROM: DR. JOSEPH PALLENI,
     ASSISTANT PRINCIPAL,
     HARRISON HIGH SCHOOL
RE: NEW HOMEROOM ASSIGNMENTS
     FOR SPRING TERM

Dear Philip\_\_\_\_,
   As we head into the Spring term, the faculty committee has made some changes in home-room assignments. This will facilitate the movements of students, as well as allow for a greater degree of freedom in the planning of Spring term extracurricular schedules.

Your new homeroom teacher is: <u>Miss Narwin</u> , in room: <u>206</u> . Effective <u>Wednesday, March 28, 8 A.M.</u>

Thank you for your cooperation.

Dr. Joseph Palleni
*Assistant Principal*

---

**8:20 P.M.**
**Phone Conversation**
**between Philip Malloy and Allison Doresett**

PHILIP MALLOY: Can I speak to Allison, please?

ALLISON DORESETT: This is she.

PHILIP MALLOY: Oh, Allison. . . . Hi. This is Phil.

ALLISON DORESETT: Phil?

PHILIP MALLOY: Philip Malloy.

ALLISON DORESETT: Oh, hi.

PHILIP MALLOY: What's happening?

ALLISON DORESETT: Not much.

PHILIP MALLOY: Must have been something you ate.

ALLISON DORESETT: Disgusting!

PHILIP MALLOY: Hey, I . . . I was wondering . . . the English exam. Next week. You know? . . .

ALLISON DORESETT: Yes?

PHILIP MALLOY: Well, I thought . . . did you read the whole thing yet? *Call of the Wild.*

**ALLISON DORESETT:** Finished it last night. We're supposed to review it all tomorrow, you know. For that exam.

**PHILIP MALLOY:** Allison . . .

**ALLISON DORESETT:** What?

**PHILIP MALLOY:** I lost my copy.

**ALLISON DORESETT:** You what?

**PHILIP MALLOY:** Wasn't my fault. See, I had this idea—I thought I'd try reading it to a dog.

**ALLISON DORESETT:** A dog!

**PHILIP MALLOY:** Well, it's about dogs, right? So I started to read it to him—this really mean dog— slobbering mouth, running eyes, the whole bit— only, see, he grabs it and starts to run away.

**ALLISON DORESETT:** This isn't true. . . .

**PHILIP MALLOY:** No, listen! Don't laugh! I'm serious! And I chased him into—I'm a runner, right?—chased him into a yard and there he was—burying the book in the ground. I couldn't get it back. The point is, *he* hated it too!

**ALLISON DORESETT:** You're too much.

**PHILIP MALLOY:** So, I have to tell Narwin I couldn't finish it.

**ALLISON DORESETT:** Right. Dare you to say that to her.

**PHILIP MALLOY:** Think I should?

**ALLISON DORESETT:** You always make remarks.

**PHILIP MALLOY:** Somebody's got to keep the class awake.

**ALLISON DORESETT:** Yeah, but, hate to tell you, I liked the book.

**PHILIP MALLOY:** Whoops! Sorry, wrong number! Goodbye!

# Chapter 4

Monday, March 19

Question four: What is the significance of Jack London's choice in making Buck, the dog in *The Call of the Wild,* the focus of his novel? Is the dog meant to be symbolic? Explain your answer. Can *people* learn from this portrayal of a dog? Expand on these ideas.

**Philip Malloy's Answer
to Exam-Question Four**

The significance of Buck in Jack London's novel *The Call of the Wild* is that Buck is symbolic of a cat. You might think that cats have nothing to do with the book, but *that* is the point. Dogs are willing to sit around and have writers write about them, which, in my personal opinion, makes them dumb. I think cats are smart. Cats don't like cold. A book that takes up so much time about a dog is pretty dumb. The book itself is a dog. That is what people can learn from Jack London's novel *The Call of the Wild.*

Philip, this is an unacceptable response. *The Call of the Wild* is an acknowledged masterpiece of American literature. You are not required to like it. You—along with your fellow students—*are* required to give it your *respectful,* thoughtful attention. In short, you are being asked to be more than lazy in your thinking.

Though your other answers are only a little better, I know you have the potential for good work. Your Fall term work showed greater promise, though your classroom attitude leaves much to be desired. Now, Philip, if you do not bring your work up, you are in danger of failing this course. When you get your Winter term grade, consider it a warning.

EXAM GRADE: C-

# Chapter 5

Tuesday, March 20

---

## MEMO

### HARRISON SCHOOL DISTRICT

Where Our Children Are Educated,
Not Just Taught

Dr. Albert Seymour  Mrs. Gloria Harland
*Superintendent* *Chairman, School Board*

TO: DR. GERTRUDE DOANE,
  PRINCIPAL, HARRISON HIGH
  SCHOOL
FROM: MARGARET NARWIN
RE: APPLICATION FOR GRANT

Attached please find my application to the State Office for Education for a summer grant-in-aid.

As you can see, I am applying to the State University for a summer program entitled "New Approaches to the Teaching of Literature for Today's Students."

It's an intensive two-week workshop in which university professors and high school "master teachers" will present new ideas, theoretical as well as practical, for the experienced high school English teacher. The application form requires both an approval and a recommendation from my head administrator, which is why I write you.

I have been teaching for a long time. Indeed, you, Dr. Doane, one of my most successful students, will know how long! I feel I am in need of new ideas, strategies, concepts to keep my teaching vital. The truth is —and I believe I can speak honestly to you about this—I feel that sometimes I am a little out of touch with contemporary teaching, and, just as important, the students who come before me these days. My love of literature—which has served me so well all these years—is perhaps not enough. I want to find new works and new ways to entice the young people of today.

In any case, you can easily see that the real beneficiaries of the program—if I am able to attend—will be the students of Harrison High.

I know how reduced and restricted district money is these days, but over the years I have not asked for this kind of support before. The State University tuition, two thousand dollars, is quite beyond my personal budget.

May I ask you to give this request your personal and immediate attention.

Sincerely,

*Peg*

Margaret Narwin

# Chapter 6

**Wednesday, March 21**

---

## MEMO

### HARRISON SCHOOL DISTRICT

Where Our Children Are Educated,
Not Just Taught

Dr. Albert Seymour    Mrs. Gloria Harland
*Superintendent*  *Chairman, School Board*

**TO: ALL ADMINISTRATORS, FACULTY, AND STAFF**

**FROM: SCHOOL SUPERINTENDENT SEYMOUR**

Dear Colleagues:

As I am sure you are well aware, the April 5 municipal elections will have voters—*for the second time*—casting ballots on the school budget. This time, in addition, a new Board of Education will be chosen.

Since the budget was rejected a month ago, we have worked very hard to cut our request for next year to the bone. But there is still no guarantee that the voters will accept this

---

budget either.

Throughout the U.S. we find that the aging population (living on restricted and/or shrinking incomes in an inflation-prone world), along with reduced government support of education, conflicts with the needs of young people who live in a society that demands educational excellence even while promoting passive acceptance of mass-media culture.

I therefore *urge* all of you to talk to as many voters as possible in an effort to make clear our vision of the educational future here in Harrison. *Let me be blunt.* A failure to win voter approval on this budget can only mean major problems for programs and personnel.

In reference to the forthcoming board elections, I should like to remind you of this: tempers can flare; hot words are often part of public debate. If, by chance, any controversial issue springs up between now and election day, I would very much appreciate being informed as to the particulars. None of us likes to be taken unawares. If this office can provide information and facts to the electorate, we shall all be better off. An informed voter is a wise voter. Let us inform the voters with the truth.

Sincerely,
Dr. Albert Seymour, D. Ed.
*School Superintendent*

# Chapter 7

Friday, March 23

Got my term grades. Math, an A. Awesome wicked. B- in biology. That's OK too. And I got a C in history, which is cool. All of that stuff is dead anyway. A straight B in health. But then I got a D in English!!! Narwin is so dumb she didn't get the joke.

I'll have to try something different with her. Maybe I should tell her how boring she is. Bad combo— boring teaching and stupid books. What she really wants us to do is put down the things *she* thinks. She wrote that on my exam paper too. Wish I hadn't thrown it out. It *was* funny. Bet Allison would have laughed. And now I'm going to get Narwin for a homeroom teacher too. *Not me.*

Worked out with Mike at the track. Short sprints. Starts. Long runs. Calmed me down. Tryouts for the team on Monday. Can't wait. I know I'll make it. Have to ask the folks to spring for those shoes.

Maybe I'll give up the paper route.

There was this neat show on TV. Really scary. About these guys in Vietnam. Or maybe it was South America. Doesn't matter. Anyway, it has all this stuff about drug fighters and Arab spies. And the Mafia.

Sarah Gloss was reading this book *The Outsiders*. Said it was the best book she ever read. Said she'd give it to me when she was done.

Saw Allison today. Did this thing. Swept off the cap. Big bow. She was trying to keep from cracking up. I'm getting to her. It's neat the way I can figure out what people think of me. Gives me a jump-start.

Tonight went out to this restaurant called Treasure Island. Seafood place. Dad loves seafood. He said I could have anything on the menu but lobster. Had a couple of hamburgers and fries. He was sore. I wish people would say what they mean.

Twenty minutes on the rowing machine.

Steve Hallick ran a mile in four seven!!!! I'd give *anything* if I could be like him.

# Chapter 8

Monday, March 26

---

### MEMO

---

#### HARRISON SCHOOL DISTRICT

Where Our Children Are Educated,
Not Just Taught

Dr. Albert Seymour  Mrs. Gloria Harland
*Superintendent* *Chairman, School Board*

TO: MARGARET NARWIN
FROM: DR. GERTRUDE DOANE,
  PRINCIPAL, HARRISON HIGH
  SCHOOL
RE: APPLICATION FOR GRANT

Dear Peg,

As much as I would like to be supportive, and while I can wholeheartedly approve of your desire to take the workshop "New Approaches to the Teaching of Literature for Today's Students," I am afraid I cannot give it formal approval.

The problem, as you may have foreseen, is severely limited district money.

---

Such funds as are available for teacher support of this nature have already been allocated. In fact, the last of them just went to Kimberly Howard, the music teacher, who will be taking a summer course in Marching Band Techniques, something that will give pleasure to so many people, and, it is hoped, encourage greater attendance at athletic events. School Superintendent Seymour is very high on sports as a community bond. Need I say more?

Finally, with a budget crisis at hand—the budget vote looms large—it's hard to plan anything at this time.

I do want to say, on a personal level, how much I admire your willingness to expand your intellectual and teaching horizons. You have always been one of our best teachers, and I know you will continue to be so. If there is any way I can facilitate your taking this course—other than with district funds—please let me know. You can always count on me.

Sincerely,

*Gert*

Dr. Gertrude Doane

PHILIP MALLOY: Coach Jamison?

COACH JAMISON: Oh, Phil. Come on in, boy. Nice to see you. Sit down. Make yourself at home.

PHILIP MALLOY: I got your note. You wanted to see me.

COACH JAMISON: Been reading about the Philadelphia Classic Track Meet.

PHILIP MALLOY: Got a great runner from this school in Pittsburgh.

COACH JAMISON: Steve Hallick?

PHILIP MALLOY: Really great. Fast. And strong.

COACH JAMISON: Sure looks it.

PHILIP MALLOY: Coach Jamison . . .

COACH JAMISON: What's that?

PHILIP MALLOY: I've been practicing every day. Working hard. I really have.

COACH JAMISON: Have you? That's great. I heard you were a hard worker. That's the way to do it. Your dad was a runner, wasn't he?

PHILIP MALLOY: Yeah. He was good. Had to quit.

COACH JAMISON: What happened?

PHILIP MALLOY: Family stuff. His father got sick or something. Couldn't stay in college.

COACH JAMISON: Yeah. It's never easy.

PHILIP MALLOY: I'm really up for the tryouts. I got some class shoes. Worked them in. I think we're going to be county champs.

COACH JAMISON: Hope so. Look, Phil, that's what I wanted to talk to you about. I've got a copy of your winter term grades here.

PHILIP MALLOY: You do?

COACH JAMISON: Well, I have to check these things. Saves problems later on. You know, there's a school rule—actually, a district rule—that you can't be on a team unless you've got a passing grade in every subject. A passing grade.

PHILIP MALLOY: A passing grade?

COACH JAMISON: Yeah. In high school. A passing grade.

PHILIP MALLOY: I didn't know.

COACH JAMISON: Well, high school . . . The point is, Phil, see, here—look—it looks like you don't have— see—all passing grades. Look here, now. There's a D here.

PHILIP MALLOY: I never heard that rule.

COACH JAMISON: In your student handbook. Read it?

PHILIP MALLOY: I don't think anyone does.

COACH JAMISON: *This* grade isn't too bad. And this grade. Fine. These. The one that really hurts is here. English. Now, if you could have gotten that up a notch. Just a bit. Even a C minus. But a D isn't— by the rules—passing. So I guess we've got a problem.

PHILIP MALLOY: We do?

COACH JAMISON: Afraid so. Look—

PHILIP MALLOY: It's Miss Narwin. I keep trying to get her to like me. She won't. She's so old-fashioned. Boring.

COACH JAMISON: Now, Phil. I know she's tough. Is there any point in your talking to her?

PHILIP MALLOY: Me?

COACH JAMISON: Sure.

PHILIP MALLOY: Could you?

COACH JAMISON: What about your doing extra work? I mean, it's no good this way.

PHILIP MALLOY: What do you mean?

COACH JAMISON: The rule . . . As it stands now, Phil—it's not me saying this, but this rule—you're not even allowed to try out. And I'm not going to kid you. This does mess with the team.

PHILIP MALLOY: Honest. I didn't know about that rule.

COACH JAMISON: Exactly. You need passing grades. See, rule's been around for a long time.

PHILIP MALLOY: No one ever told me. And I'm practicing every day.

COACH JAMISON: Sure—

PHILIP MALLOY: It's so unfair.

COACH JAMISON: Well, in high school—

PHILIP MALLOY: I mean, you can't kid around with her or anything.

**COACH JAMISON:** Phil, if there is one thing sports teaches—and I'm always saying this—all the guys will tell you—sometimes you have to go along to get along. That's the whole thing about sports. Go with the flow.

**PHILIP MALLOY:** I think it's a personal thing with her. It really is. She has it in for me. I mean, I shouldn't be in her class. Could you get me switched?

**COACH JAMISON:** Maybe if you talked to her. Do some catch-up work. How about it? Promise to hit the books. Extra stuff. Bet you could. Look, everything I've heard suggests you are fast. Real potential. This is a big disappointment.

**PHILIP MALLOY:** I mean, if I knew it was a rule—

**COACH JAMISON:** Yeah. One thing sports teaches. A rule is a rule. It isn't always easy.

**PHILIP MALLOY:** I didn't know.

**COACH JAMISON:** Well, thing is, now you do.

---

**1:30 P.M.**
**Discussion in**
**Margaret Narwin's English Class**

---

**MISS NARWIN:** Now, class, during the first few weeks of this new term we'll be reading William Shakespeare's *Julius Caesar*. How many of you have ever read a play by Shakespeare before? Well, then, you're in for a treat. You are not an educated person unless you have read Shakespeare. Philip?

**PHILIP MALLOY:** What?

**MISS NARWIN:** I'd rather you look up at me, not out the window.

**PHILIP MALLOY:** I was listening.

**MISS NARWIN:** Can you repeat what I said?

**PHILIP MALLOY:** We're reading something.

**MISS NARWIN:** William Shakespeare.

**PHILIP MALLOY:** Whatever you say.

**MISS NARWIN:** Philip, I think I've suggested before that your comments can be tiresome. Now, please, try to stay with me.

**PHILIP MALLOY:** Yeah.

# Chapter 9

Tuesday, March 27

**6:23 P.M.**
**Discussion**
**between Philip Malloy's Parents**

MRS. MALLOY: Honey, did you have a chance to look at Phil's grades?

MR. MALLOY: What?

MRS. MALLOY: Did you look at Phil's grades. I left them on the bureau.

MR. MALLOY: Uh, yes. Where is he?

MRS. MALLOY: In the basement. On your rowing machine.

MR. MALLOY: Should use that thing more myself. Putting on weight.

MRS. MALLOY: You certainly are. Did you?

MR. MALLOY: I'm looking at them now.

MRS. MALLOY: What do you think?

MR. MALLOY: Not too bad. Except for English. What's the problem there?

MRS. MALLOY: He says it's the teacher.

**MR. MALLOY:** I've seen him read.

**MRS. MALLOY:** He's reading some paperback. *Insiders. Outsiders.* I don't know. Some girl gave it to him. That doesn't seem to be the problem.

**MR. MALLOY:** I never was one for reading much. I mean, other than sports. Course now, papers. Too much of that.

**MRS. MALLOY:** Ben, he could flunk that course.

**MR. MALLOY:** Won't be the end of the world. What would he have to do, go to summer school? Maybe that's the lesson he needs. Kids only do what they want to do.

**MRS. MALLOY:** The last couple of days he's been very moody.

**MR. MALLOY:** Come on. He's fourteen.

**MRS. MALLOY:** He doesn't want to talk. To me, anyway. Maybe you should be spending more time with him.

**MR. MALLOY:** I know. All tied up in this—

**MRS. MALLOY:** I understand. But work's better, isn't it?

**MR. MALLOY:** Some. Did he make the track team?

**MRS. MALLOY:** You know, I completely forgot to ask him. Maybe that's the problem.

**MR. MALLOY:** I'll talk to him.

**MRS. MALLOY:** Do you know—about a week ago, he asked me if we—you and I—were getting a divorce?

**MR. MALLOY:** *What?*

MRS. MALLOY: Really.

MR. MALLOY: How'd he come up with that?

MRS. MALLOY: I'm not sure. Maybe he'd overheard. . . . I told him bickering happens in a marriage. It's perfectly normal. Life isn't a sitcom.

MR. MALLOY: Right. The real world doesn't have a laugh track.

---

**8:50 P.M.**
**Discussion**
**between Philip Malloy and His Father**

---

MR. MALLOY: Can I talk to you?

PHILIP MALLOY: Sure

MR. MALLOY: How much time you spending on this?

PHILIP MALLOY: Few times a day. Short sprints.

MR. MALLOY: Like I'm always telling you, just make sure you warm up each time. But it's good for the back. Helps with starts.

PHILIP MALLOY: I know.

MR. MALLOY: Uh, Phil . . . School stuff. Straight up. What's the story in English?

PHILIP MALLOY: What do you mean?

MR. MALLOY: I saw your grades. Most of them are decent. What's with English?

PHILIP MALLOY: I can speak it.

MR. MALLOY: Seriously. . . .

PHILIP MALLOY: You want the truth?

MR. MALLOY: Sure. Well?

PHILIP MALLOY: It's the teacher, Narwin.

MR. MALLOY: What do you mean?

PHILIP MALLOY: She has it in for me.

MR. MALLOY: How come?

PHILIP MALLOY: I don't know. Nobody likes her. People don't do well in her classes. Except her favorites.

MR. MALLOY: Want me or your ma to go in and talk to her?

PHILIP MALLOY: I can handle her.

MR. MALLOY: What are you reading in school?

PHILIP MALLOY: *Julius Caesar.* Shakespeare.

MR. MALLOY: Uh-oh.

PHILIP MALLOY: *So* bad. This Narwin has us reading these tiny bits every night, but *no one* understands it. I mean it, *no one!!!* She says it's English, but it must have been English before English got there. At least it's not any English I've ever heard.

MR. MALLOY: Well, reading is important.

PHILIP MALLOY: I read. Ever hear of *The Outsiders?* It's about these guys—they live alone—without parents.

MR. MALLOY: Think I saw it on cable. How you getting on with the track team? Phil?

PHILIP MALLOY: I, ah . . . was thinking I wouldn't try out.

MR. MALLOY: Come again?

PHILIP MALLOY: Thinking of not trying out.

MR. MALLOY: You kidding?

PHILIP MALLOY: No.

MR. MALLOY: But high school track is . . . Why?

PHILIP MALLOY: Lot of reasons.

MR. MALLOY: Like what?

PHILIP MALLOY: Dad . . .

MR. MALLOY: I want to know.

PHILIP MALLOY: Just because you did it doesn't mean I have to.

MR. MALLOY: Now, wait a minute. You're really into it. We just got you new shoes. And you're good. Better than I ever was. You *are*. I love watching you run. You shouldn't give it up. And here you are working out. I don't get it. What's going on?

PHILIP MALLOY: Nothing.

MR. MALLOY: Didn't you tell me the coach *asked* you to be on the team?

PHILIP MALLOY: Doesn't mean—

MR. MALLOY: Phil, I don't get it.

PHILIP MALLOY: It's my choice.

MR. MALLOY: Phil, let me tell you something. If God gives you a ticket, you better use it.

PHILIP MALLOY: Ticket to what?

MR. MALLOY: Running.

PHILIP MALLOY: I'll think about it.

MR. MALLOY: Those shoes weren't cheap either. Real first-class stuff. I mean, I don't understand. I thought you were ready for it.

PHILIP MALLOY: Come on, Dad. I'm not you.

---

**9:24 P.M.**
**From a Letter Written by Margaret Narwin
to Her Sister, Anita Wigham**

---

. . . Anita, the truth is I'm hurt. *Never* in all the years I've been at Harrison have I asked for *anything* in the way of extra funds. If it were a case of *no* money available for *anyone,* why, I could accept that. But, no, a certain Kimberly Howard, who had been here for only *two* years, and who has a husband who works for some large corporation, *she* received money! And for some idiotic course in marching-band music! It makes me *outraged* to think about it.

What has happened to our society? Where are its values?

I suppose marching bands make a big show. Bread and circuses, Anita. Bread and circuses. That's all it is. I don't think I've ever been so angry!

I think there's a question of fairness here. That old-fashioned word *respect*—how often Mother used it!—occurs to me often these days. Call it pride, call it vanity, but I would like some respect for all I have done here. From the community. From the administration. Yes, from the *students*. I work hard for them!

The truth is it's our superintendent's doing. There is a second budget vote coming up. I told you the first one failed. He sent out a memo to everybody warning us that it might fail again. Almost a threat. He is a *very* political person. But then, all he wants is to keep *his* job.

Oh, I am so angry. . . .

Folks got my grades. Ma asked me a few things about them before supper. I didn't say much. Then, afterward, Dad talked to me. About the grades. Wasn't that he blew his stack or anything. I told him the truth. He seemed to understand. But then he asked me about my being on the track team. Didn't know what to say. If I told him what happened he would have been really mad. So I just said I decided I wouldn't go for the tryouts.

That got him upset.

I just realized two things that make me want to puke. Track practice starts tomorrow and I'm not on the team. Also, I start homeroom with *Narwin!!!!!* Can't stand even looking at her. I have to find a way to get transferred out.

MRS. MALLOY: Did you talk to Philip? About that grade?

MR. MALLOY: Sure.

MRS. MALLOY: What's going on?

MR. MALLOY: I'm not sure. Fussing with the English teacher.

MRS. MALLOY: What do you mean?

MR. MALLOY: Like he told you. He doesn't like her. I told him he didn't have much choice. Take the bad with the good. Then he said he wasn't going to try out for track.

**MRS. MALLOY:** That he was *not?*

**MR. MALLOY:** That's what he told me.

**MRS. MALLOY:** But that's all he thinks about.

**MR. MALLOY:** I know. He doesn't know how good he is. I reminded him.

**MRS. MALLOY:** Did he give a reason?

**MR. MALLOY:** Not really. Something about not having to do what I did.

**MRS. MALLOY:** Oh, he'll change his mind. Kids are so moody.

**MR. MALLOY:** Hope so.

**MRS. MALLOY:** Maybe just don't mention it.

**MR. MALLOY:** Maybe.

**MRS. MALLOY:** I'm glad you spoke to him. Not every father would.

**MR. MALLOY:** He doesn't make it easy.

# Chapter 10

## Wednesday, March 28

---

**7:30 A.M.**
**Conversation**
**between Philip Malloy and Ken Barchet**
**on the Way to the School Bus**

---

**PHILIP MALLOY:** What's happening, man?

**KEN BARCHET:** Nothing. Got room changes. Who'd you get?

**PHILIP MALLOY:** Narwin.

**KEN BARCHET:** So do I. She's okay.

**PHILIP MALLOY:** Can't stand her.

**KEN BARCHET:** Doesn't matter. It's just homeroom.

**PHILIP MALLOY:** No way. I've got her for English too. I'm going to get transferred out of both.

**KEN BARCHET:** Why?

**PHILIP MALLOY:** Told you. Can't stand her.

**KEN BARCHET:** How you going to do that?

**PHILIP MALLOY:** I'm working on it.

**KEN BARCHET:** Sure . . . Malloy Magic, right?

**PHILIP MALLOY:** You'll see.

MISS NARWIN: Ladies and gentlemen, please settle down. All right. Settle down. For the moment just take any seat you wish. We'll work out particular problems a bit later on. Yes?

STUDENT: Am I supposed to be in this room?

MISS NARWIN: What's your name?

STUDENT: Lisa Gibbons.

MISS NARWIN: Lisa? Yes, you're on my list. Just take any seat for the moment.

STUDENT: Miss Narwin, what about me?

MISS NARWIN: Is that you, Gloria? No, you're not here. Did you get a notice?

GLORIA: No.

MISS NARWIN: Oh, dear. Best check in the main office.

ALLISON DORESETT: What about me?

MISS NARWIN: You'll all have to lower your voices if I'm going to sort things out. Yes, Allison, you are here. Yes?

STUDENT: Joseph R. Rippens.

MISS NARWIN: I think that—

INTERCOM VOICE OF DR. GERTRUDE DOANE, HARRISON HIGH PRINCIPAL: Good morning to all students, faculty, and staff.

STUDENT: Am I?

MISS NARWIN: Please, let's just get done with the morning business.

DR. DOANE: Today is Wednesday, March 28. Today will be a Schedule B day.

Today in history: in the year A.D. 193 the Roman Emperor Pertinax was assassinated. On this day in 1862 the Civil War battle of Glorieta, New Mexico, was fought. Today in Czechoslovakia it is Teachers' Day.

Please all rise and stand at respectful, silent attention for the playing of our national anthem.

*Oh, say, can you see by the dawn's early light . . .*

MISS NARWIN: Is that someone humming?

*What so proudly we hailed at the twilight's last gleaming?*

*Whose broad stripes and bright stars . . .*

MISS NARWIN: I don't know who that is, but you heard Dr. Doane request silence.

*. . . thro' the perilous fight,*

*O'er the ramparts we watched were so gallantly streaming? . . .*

MISS NARWIN: Is that you, Philip?

*And the rockets' red glare, the bombs bursting in air . . .*

PHILIP MALLOY: Just humming.

MISS NARWIN: Please stop it.

*Gave proof thro' the night that our flag was still there. . . .*

PHILIP MALLOY: Mr. Lunser doesn't mind. I just—

MISS NARWIN: Stop it now.

PHILIP MALLOY: But—

*Oh, say does that star-spangled banner yet wave . . .*

MISS NARWIN: Now! Thank you.

*O'er the land of the free and the home of the brave?*

---

**10:30 A.M.**
**Discussion between Margaret Narwin and
Jacob Benison, Science Teacher,
in the Faculty Room**

---

MR. BENISON: Morning, Peg. How's it going? Lots of confusion with the new homerooms?

MISS NARWIN: I'll get through it.

MR. BENISON: Awful lot of mix-ups. Kids going every which way. As if they weren't informed. Happens this way every year. Sometimes I think it's not worth the trouble.

MISS NARWIN: I agree.

MR. BENISON: I'll be glad to get out of it. Forty-four more days!

MISS NARWIN: Sometimes I think I should join you.

MR. BENISON: Can't wait. Get you some coffee? Kim brought in muffins.

MISS NARWIN: Kim?

MR. BENISON: Kimberly Howard. Music.

MISS NARWIN: I'll just sit here.

MR. BENISON: Something the matter, Peg?

MISS NARWIN: Oh, stupid business. I suppose it's this changing homeroom classes. The announcements, and so on. And when the national anthem comes on, the students *are* supposed to stand in silence.

MR. BENISON: Right. "Respect, silence, and attention," I think the rule reads.

MISS NARWIN: Exactly. I had a student who started to hum loudly. Very loudly.

MR. BENISON: Uh-oh. Who was that?

MISS NARWIN: Philip Malloy.

MR. BENISON: Oh, sure, Phil. Nice kid. Bright—when he gets around to doing some work. Which isn't exactly every day. He's got being fast on his brain. Humming loudly? What was he doing that for?

MISS NARWIN: I don't know. I had to ask him to stop.

MR. BENISON: Did he?

MISS NARWIN: Not at first. I spoke to him twice. He claimed he always did it before.

MR. BENISON: That right?

MISS NARWIN: Bernie Lunser's class.

MR. BENISON: Oh? Well, the term won't last forever.

MISS NARWIN: Sometimes I wonder. Maybe I will get some coffee.

MR. BENISON: Hey, the meaning of life!

12:15 P.M.
**Discussion
between Philip Malloy and Todd Becker
in the School Lunchroom**

**TODD BECKER:** Hey, man, how come you aren't going out for track?

**PHILIP MALLOY:** Got too much to do.

**TODD BECKER:** We could use you, man. Need some power. We really could.

**PHILIP MALLOY:** I'll think about it.

**TODD BECKER:** You should.

**PHILIP MALLOY:** Just don't bug me.

**TODD BECKER:** Sure. Sure. I'm just asking. Who'd you get for homeroom?

**PHILIP MALLOY:** What?

**TODD BECKER:** Who's your new homeroom teacher?

**PHILIP MALLOY:** Narwin.

**TODD BECKER:** I like her.

**PHILIP MALLOY:** I hate her.

**TODD BECKER:** Yeah? How come?

**PHILIP MALLOY:** She is the stupidest teacher. . . . You know how they play "The Star-Spangled Banner" in the morning . . . ?

**TODD BECKER:** Yeah. . . .

**PHILIP MALLOY:** Well, I started to sing it. . . .

TODD BECKER: Why?

PHILIP MALLOY: Felt like it.

TODD BECKER: So?

PHILIP MALLOY: She told me to stop.

TODD BECKER: Stop what?

PHILIP MALLOY: Humming.

TODD BECKER: Thought you said singing.

PHILIP MALLOY: Whatever.

TODD BECKER: How come she made you stop?

PHILIP MALLOY: I don't know. She's got something against me. I don't know what it is. She really has it in for me. Something. I mean, she's always onto me about something. Really. I wish I knew.

TODD BECKER: What did you do?

PHILIP MALLOY: I told you. Nothing.

TODD BECKER: No. I mean when she told you to stop humming.

PHILIP MALLOY: I stopped.

TODD BECKER: Man, those are the biggest cookies I ever saw. Like pizzas.

PHILIP MALLOY: My mother makes them.

TODD BECKER: Amazing.

PHILIP MALLOY: Here. Take a piece. Humming, would you believe it? No way I'm staying in her classes.

**MISS NARWIN:** Now, scene two, line fifty-two. Brutus says, "No, Cassius; for the eye sees not itself / But by reflection, by some other things." What does he mean by that? Anyone? Someone want to take a chance? Roger?

**ROGER SANCHEZ:** That he can't see himself.

**MISS NARWIN:** Close. Yes, Philip?

**PHILIP MALLOY:** Yeah, but what if he's cross-eyed? He'd see himself then, wouldn't he?

**MISS NARWIN:** Philip, I'm not even going to respond to that! Terri?

**3:15 P.M.**
**Discussion**
**between Philip Malloy and Allison Doresett**
**on the School Bus**

**ALLISON DORESETT:** Can I sit next to you?

**PHILIP MALLOY:** Oh, sure. Sure.

**ALLISON DORESETT:** What's the matter? You look like death warmed over.

**PHILIP MALLOY:** I'm okay.

**ALLISON DORESETT:** You got Miss Narwin mad with that joke in English.

**PHILIP MALLOY:** She's always mad at me.

ALLISON DORESETT: Is something the matter?

PHILIP MALLOY: Nothing.

ALLISON DORESETT: School was so frantic today.

PHILIP MALLOY: Yeah.

ALLISON DORESETT: All the sports and stuff. Hey, how come you didn't go to track tryouts?

PHILIP MALLOY: Had to do something.

ALLISON DORESETT: Todd said you were really great. That with you on the team we were going to be county champs.

PHILIP MALLOY: Yeah.

ALLISON DORESETT: Boy, you're in a mood!

PHILIP MALLOY: Just don't feel like talking.

ALLISON DORESETT: Well excuse me!

PHILIP MALLOY: Hey, Allison, wait . . . Damn!

---

**3:20 P.M.**
**Discussion between**
**Margaret Narwin and Bernard Lunser**
**Outside the School's Main Office**

---

MISS NARWIN: Bernie!

MR. LUNSER: Oh, hi, Peg. How you doing?

MISS NARWIN: Fine. I need to ask you something.

MR. LUNSER: What's that?

MISS NARWIN: In your morning homeroom . . .

MR. LUNSER: Yeah?

MISS NARWIN: When the national anthem is played . . .

MR. LUNSER: Right . . .

MISS NARWIN: Do you allow your students to sing along?

MR. LUNSER: *Sing?*

MISS NARWIN: During the national anthem.

MR. LUNSER: Ummmmmm . . . I thought the kids are supposed to be quiet.

MISS NARWIN: One of my new homeroom students, Philip Malloy, informed me that you always allowed singing.

MR. LUNSER: Oh, Philip . . . Right. He was in my homeroom. He'd do better if he thought himself a little less clever and got his brain into something besides running. But I like him. A decent kid. You get him?

MISS NARWIN: Do you allow singing?

MR. LUNSER: Singing?

MISS NARWIN: Yes.

MR. LUNSER: The rule says keep quiet . . .

MISS NARWIN: But do you allow singing?

MR. LUNSER: Hey, Peg, do I look like a guy who goes around breaking important rules?

MISS NARWIN: Thanks.

**MRS. MALLOY:** You seem very quiet tonight, Philip. Want some more gravy?

**PHILIP MALLOY:** I've got enough.

**MR. MALLOY:** I'll have some. What did you decide to do about the track team?

**MRS. MALLOY:** Philip, your father asked you something.

**PHILIP MALLOY:** What?

**MR. MALLOY:** I asked you a question. You still not going out for track?

**MRS. MALLOY:** Philip, is something the matter?

**PHILIP MALLOY:** I'm not on the team.

**MR. MALLOY:** I know that's what you said. But I'd like to know why. Something must be the matter.

**PHILIP MALLOY:** What would you say . . .

**MRS. MALLOY:** Phil, don't talk with your mouth full.

**MR. MALLOY:** Have I *ever* missed one of your meets? Ever? This boy is the best runner in town. Makes me feel proud.

**MRS. MALLOY:** Ben, we know that. What were you saying, Phil?

**PHILIP MALLOY:** What would you say if a teacher said I wasn't allowed to sing "The Star-Spangled Banner?"

**MR. MALLOY:** What?

**PHILIP MALLOY:** Singing "The Star-Spangled Banner."

**MR. MALLOY:** Anywhere?

**PHILIP MALLOY:** In class.

**MRS. MALLOY:** I don't understand. What's this have to do with what your father asked—your running? Singing in the middle of class?

**PHILIP MALLOY:** Ma, listen! I'm trying to tell you. I mean . . . you know, when school starts, first period, homeroom, when they play, you know, the . . . song over the speaker system. It's a tape.

**MR. MALLOY:** Come again.

**PHILIP MALLOY:** I'm trying to explain!

**MR. MALLOY:** No need to raise your voice!

**MRS. MALLOY:** The both of you . . .

**MR. MALLOY:** Now, Philip, just tell us what—obviously, something has happened. Calmly and factually, tell us what happened. Why you are so upset?

**PHILIP MALLOY:** I told you. . . . In school today . . .

**MR. MALLOY:** Okay. In school today. But what?

**PHILIP MALLOY:** We got new homeroom teachers.

**MRS. MALLOY:** Just you?

**PHILIP MALLOY:** No. I never said that. Everybody. The whole school.

**MRS. MALLOY:** I don't understand.

**MR. MALLOY:** Susan, just let Phil tell his story without interruptions.

MRS. MALLOY: I'm just trying to understand.

PHILIP MALLOY: Anyway, I got this Miss Narwin. She's a real bitch. . . .

MR. MALLOY: Phil!

PHILIP MALLOY: Do you want to know what happened or not!

MRS. MALLOY: Honey, let the boy tell it his way.

PHILIP MALLOY: Anyway, they always start off the day, you know, with playing "The Star-Spangled Banner." Okay. It's stupid, but, well, sometimes I sort of sing along. . . .

MRS. MALLOY: You have a very sweet voice.

PHILIP MALLOY: Or hum. . . .

MR. MALLOY: Hum?

PHILIP MALLOY: Yeah. Right. Hum. No big deal. But this teacher, she got real mad and started to yell at me to stop.

MRS. MALLOY: She yelled?

PHILIP MALLOY: Yeah.

MR. MALLOY: Let me understand this. Just—out of the blue—she yelled at you because you were—?

PHILIP MALLOY: Right. Humming. That's all I was doing, I mean, not loud. Soft.

MR. MALLOY: And she yelled at you?

PHILIP MALLOY: That's what I'm trying to say.

MRS. MALLOY: That's not what I'd call fair.

**MR. MALLOY:** The national anthem— "Oh, say, can you see"—is that what you're talking about?

**PHILIP MALLOY:** Yeah.

**MR. MALLOY:** You have some more of that . . . ?

**MRS. MALLOY:** Yams. Sweet yams.

**MR. MALLOY:** Thanks. They're delicious. Now where is he going?

**MRS. MALLOY:** He was trying to talk, and you weren't listening to him. Ben, you have to be more supportive!

**MR. MALLOY:** What do you mean?

**MRS. MALLOY:** Maybe that's why he isn't running. Maybe he's sending a message.

**MR. MALLOY:** Like what?

**MRS. MALLOY:** That he needs your support on something that isn't track. That's him.

**MR. MALLOY:** Think so?

**MRS. MALLOY:** I don't know. Just trying to understand.

**MR. MALLOY:** My day wasn't so great either.

**MRS. MALLOY:** Oh?

**MR. MALLOY:** Remember that bid we put in on that Colfax job? . . .

. . . I do think it's quite the best thing Barbara Pym ever wrote. It's one of those books about which— even as I neared the end—I said to myself, "I can't wait to read this again."

In any case, it was so soothing to come home to that quiet, thoughtful, civilized British world. Oh, Anita, I *long* to return to England someday, and those wonderful, leisurely late-afternoon cream teas. . . .

The truth is, I needed a soothing. Today was "Spring Changeover Day," when our students, after six months of struggling to learn exactly where to go, are suddenly tossed pell-mell here, there, anywhere, as their schedules and homeroom assignments shift because of spring recreational schedules. Of course, bedlam is always the result, with attendant bad feeling. It's just at those moments that students rear up and challenge your authority. One has to be vigilant and *firm*. As well as consistent and fair. That's the key with students these days. And sometimes I haven't the stamina for it. Ah, well . . .

Thank you for passing on the kind words of Mr. Chevers. Of course I remember him . . .

Today was rotten. Nothing was right. I felt like punching Narwin in the face. It all just stinks.

**ALLISON DORESETT:** Oh, on the bus coming home, you know, I was going to sit with Phil Malloy.

**JANET BARSKY:** You like him, don't you?

**ALLISON DORESETT:** He's kind of cute. And usually really funny. But he looked upset today. Angry.

**JANET BARSKY:** How come?

**ALLISON DORESETT:** I don't know. He was that way in class too. I tried to talk to him, but he wouldn't. Anyway, I didn't sit with him.

**JANET BARSKY:** Who'd you sit with?

**ALLISON DORESETT:** Todd Becker.

**JANET BARSKY:** Todd! Too cool! He's the cutest guy!

**ALLISON DORESETT:** I know. . . . And he *always* makes me laugh.

10:45 P.M.
**Conversation
between Philip Malloy and His Father**

**MR. MALLOY:** Phil? You up? Can I speak to you?

**PHILIP MALLOY:** Oh, sure. Just reading.

**MR. MALLOY:** What're you reading?

**PHILIP MALLOY:** *The Outsiders.*

MR. MALLOY: Still?

PHILIP MALLOY: It's pretty long.

MR. MALLOY: Can I sit down?

PHILIP MALLOY: Sure.

MR. MALLOY: Now, look, this business about, you know, what you were saying at dinner, not being allowed to sing the national anthem . . .

PHILIP MALLOY: I was humming.

MR. MALLOY: Whatever. Now, your mother and I talked about this. I mean, I want you to understand—whatever it is—we're on your side.

PHILIP MALLOY: I didn't think you were interested.

MR. MALLOY: Of course I'm interested. I'm always cheering on your side.

PHILIP MALLOY: It's just that the teacher—

MR. MALLOY: No, wait. Straight up. I think she's wrong. No two ways about it. You're right to be bugged. She shouldn't put you down like that. You know, I'm—your mother and I—we're no great, well, you know, no big patriots. I don't think we even own a flag. But that doesn't mean we don't love our country. Believe me. We just don't make a big thing about it. It's not that kind of showy thing with us. But not being allowed to sing "The Star-Spangled Banner" . . . Well, that's like, sort of, not being allowed to, you know, pray. A personal thing. And the personal thing, in America . . . the point is, it doesn't seem right. And we just want you to know we're with you. It's important to us that you know that.

PHILIP MALLOY: Thanks.

MR. MALLOY: Your mother says to be more supportive. Well, sure. I mean, I'll stand with you. You never have to worry about that.

PHILIP MALLOY: You're not mad?

MR. MALLOY: Of course not. I have half a mind to talk to Ted.

PHILIP MALLOY: Why?

MR. MALLOY: He's running for school board. Election soon. I mean, Ted Griffen *is* our neighbor. That can mean something.

PHILIP MALLOY: He was always chasing me off his lawn.

MR. MALLOY: Yeah. But you were a kid then. Phil, let me tell you something. One thing I've learned is this: you really have to stick up for your rights. We'll stand with you. Don't worry. See you at breakfast.

PHILIP MALLOY: Right.

MR. MALLOY: Night, kid.

PHILIP MALLOY: Night.

MR. MALLOY: Remember. You stick up for your rights. I'll be there.

# 11

## Thursday, March 29

---

**8:02 A.M.**
**Discussion**
**in Margaret Narwin's Homeroom Class**

---

MISS NARWIN: Ladies and gentlemen, please take your seats. Your assigned seats. I need to take attendance.

STUDENT: Miss Narwin.

MISS NARWIN: Yes?

STUDENT: Peggy Lord is sick.

MISS NARWIN: Thank you.

INTERCOM VOICE OF DR. GERTRUDE DOANE, HARRISON HIGH PRINCIPAL: Good morning to all students, faculty, and staff. Today is Thursday, March 29. Today will be a Schedule A day.

Today in history: in the year 1790 our tenth president, John Tyler, was born. In 1918 singer Pearl Bailey was born. And today in 1954 Karen Ann Quinlan was born.

Please all rise and stand at respectful, silent attention for the playing of our national anthem.

*Oh, say, can you see by the dawn's early light . . .*

**MISS NARWIN:** Is that someone humming?

*What so proudly we hailed at the twilight's last gleaming?*

*Whose broad stripes and bright stars . . .*

**MISS NARWIN:** Philip, is that you again?

*. . . thro' the perilous fight,*

*O'er the ramparts we watched were so gallantly streaming? . . .*

**MISS NARWIN:** Philip, I spoke to you yesterday about this.

*And the rockets' red glare, the bombs bursting in air . . .*

**MISS NARWIN:** This is a time for listening. Now, please, stop singing.

*Gave proof thro' the night that our flag was still there. . . .*

**MISS NARWIN:** Philip, stop this insolence!

*Oh, say does that star-spangled banner yet wave*

*O'er the land of the free and the home of the brave?*

**MISS NARWIN:** Philip, leave this room instantly. Report to Dr. Palleni's office. Now!

DR. PALLENI: Okay, Philip, come on in. Sit yourself down. Who's your homeroom teacher?

PHILIP MALLOY: Miss Narwin.

DR. PALLENI: Okay. Now, what seems to be the problem?

PHILIP MALLOY: I don't know.

DR. PALLENI: Come on, Phil. Sit up straight. We don't whip people here. Now, you must have some idea. She asked you to leave the class. What happened?

PHILIP MALLOY: She doesn't like me.

DR. PALLENI: Let's try to be more specific, Philip. I want to hear your side of the problem. I'll check with her. Then, let's see if we can work something out. We're into solving problems, not making them. Okay. Now, what happened?

PHILIP MALLOY: She wouldn't let me sing "The Star-Spangled Banner."

DR. PALLENI: What?

PHILIP MALLOY: She won't let me sing "The Star-Spangled Banner."

DR. PALLENI: I don't understand.

PHILIP MALLOY: It's just a thing I like to do. Sing along when the song is played.

DR. PALLENI: "The Star-Spangled Banner"?

**PHILIP MALLOY:** Yeah. I just like to do it. In Mr. Lunser's—

**DR. PALLENI:** You mean—when the morning tape plays . . . ?

**PHILIP MALLOY:** Yeah.

**DR. PALLENI:** And you were singing?

**PHILIP MALLOY:** Uh-huh.

**DR. PALLENI:** What, loudly? Disrespectfully? Were you making fun?

**PHILIP MALLOY:** No. Not at all. Just, you know, sort of to myself. Almost humming. Really. I always do.

**DR. PALLENI:** There's a rule about being quiet at that time.

**PHILIP MALLOY:** Yeah, well, it's sort of a . . . patriotic thing with me. But the whole thing is, she always has it in for me.

**DR. PALLENI:** Who?

**PHILIP MALLOY:** Narwin. So, she kicked me out.

**DR. PALLENI:** This singing you were doing . . . singing out loud. Did Miss Narwin ask you to stop?

**PHILIP MALLOY:** I mean, I wasn't being loud or anything like that.

**DR. PALLENI:** And did you? Stop, I mean.

**PHILIP MALLOY:** No, I told you. I was singing.

**DR. PALLENI:** But, when she—Miss Narwin—asked you, did you stop?

**PHILIP MALLOY:** It was just to myself. Not loud or anything, and—

**DR. PALLENI:** Okay, okay, Phil. I think I understand now. No problem. Where is that thing? . . . Here it is. This is a memo from Dr. Doane. Look, see what it says. Go on, read it. What does it say? *Silent.* Okay? You hear it every day. Right? But you were singing. Right? No, let me finish. Miss Narwin asked you to stop. You didn't. You continued to sing. You were disobedient. So she asked you to leave.

**PHILIP MALLOY:** How can you ask someone not to sing "The Star Spangled Banner"?

**DR. PALLENI:** It's the rule.

**PHILIP MALLOY:** Is a memo a rule?

**DR. PALLENI:** Philip . . .

**PHILIP MALLOY:** Yeah, but . . .

**DR. PALLENI:** Philip, look. I've got more important things to do with my time than argue with you about following simple, basic rules. I've got serious infractions. I've got drugs. I've got—

**PHILIP MALLOY:** Put me in another homeroom.

**DR. PALLENI:** What?

**PHILIP MALLOY:** Put me in another homeroom. And another English class.

**DR. PALLENI:** What's English have to do with this? Philip, I asked you something.

**PHILIP MALLOY:** She and I don't get along.

**DR. PALLENI:** Look, Phil, you are here to get an education. To get along you have to go along. Let's not make a big deal over this, okay, Phil? Now, you've given me your side of the story. I'll check with Miss Narwin, but it seems pretty clear to me. . . . You said yourself, you broke a rule—

**PHILIP MALLOY:** If you could just change . . .

**DR. PALLENI:** Here's a note that says I spoke to you. Scoot. Get along with your day. Make it a good one.

**PHILIP MALLOY:** But . . .

**DR. PALLENI:** Hey, Phil, be cool. It's a good day. I heard you're a runner. It's a great day for running. Go join the track team. They could use you. Okay? Now, take it easy. See you around. Bye. Have a nice day.

---

**1:35 P.M.**
**Conversation**
**between Mr. Malloy and His Boss,**
**Mr. Dexter**

---

**MR. DEXTER:** Look, Ben, it was just a botched job, that's all. There are no two ways around it.

**MR. MALLOY:** Mr. Dexter, what I'm simply trying to explain is that I wasn't given all the information that would allow me—

**MR. DEXTER:** I don't want to hear excuses, Ben. I want someone around here to accept responsibility. Is that you or not?

**MR. MALLOY:** Yes, sir.

**MR. DEXTER:** It goes with your position. Responsibility. Just don't let it happen again. We lost a lot of money on this one. We can't afford it. No one should know that better than you.

**MR. MALLOY:** Yes, sir.

**MR. DEXTER:** Okay, that's all that needs to be said. It's done. We'll work around it.

**MR. MALLOY:** Yes, sir.

**MR. DEXTER:** Regular sales-reps meeting tomorrow morning. I don't intend to bring this up. But it will be on my mind. We can't afford another screwup.

**MR. MALLOY:** Yes, sir.

---

**3:35 P.M.**
**Conversation between**
**Margaret Narwin and Dr. Gertrude Doane,**
**Principal, Harrison High**

---

**DR. DOANE:** Come in, Peg. Come in.

**MISS NARWIN:** Thank you.

**DR. DOANE:** Do sit down. Would you like some coffee?

**MISS NARWIN:** No, thank you.

**DR. DOANE:** Peg, ever since you sent me that note about funds for that summer teaching workshop, I've been meaning to speak to you.

**MISS NARWIN:** You're very busy.

**DR. DOANE:** Busy? Good grief. Superintendent Seymour has us writing position papers, speaking to chamber of commerce groups . . . the Rotary club. The upcoming budget vote. He's very nervous about it. And the board election. But that's something else. You don't want to hear about that. Many is the time I wish I were back in the classroom. Though, actually, it was while doing some statistics for this budget vote business that I was able to pull something together that's interesting.

**MISS NARWIN:** Yes?

**DR. DOANE:** You know how, in your memo, you spoke of going to that workshop—that some of the instructors were—what?—"master teachers."

**MISS NARWIN:** Yes.

**DR. DOANE:** Wish we had that program here. The point is, Peg, you are the one who should be a master teacher.

**MISS NARWIN:** Thank you, but . . .

**DR. DOANE:** I mean, what I came up with is this. . . . There is a direct statistical tie-in—that is, those students who have taken an English class with you, Peg, score higher on the Iowa tests, the Stanfords, and the SAT verbals.

**MISS NARWIN:** Is that right?

**DR. DOANE:** No question. I could show you the figures.

**MISS NARWIN:** Well, that's nice to know.

**DR. DOANE:** I felt so bad about not being able to give you that funding. But, Peg, if the truth be known . . . you don't need it. You—the facts are there for all to see—you are our best English teacher. I didn't have to be told that. But there's the truth for the rest of the world to see.

**MISS NARWIN:** Thank you, Gert. I really appreciate that. I really do.

MRS. MALLOY: Hi, honey.

MR. MALLOY: 'Lo.

MRS. MALLOY: What's the matter? Something wrong?

MR. MALLOY: Got chewed out by Dexter.

MRS. MALLOY: What for?

MR. MALLOY: Some job estimate that went wrong.
Wasn't even anything I did.

MRS. MALLOY: I hope you stood up for yourself.

MR. MALLOY: Are you kidding?

MRS. MALLOY: But, honey, if you were right . . .

MR. MALLOY: And get myself in his bad books.

MRS. MALLOY: You wouldn't get yourself—

MR. MALLOY: Susan, please don't bug me about it. I
know when to keep my mouth shut.

MRS. MALLOY: But—

MR. MALLOY: You don't understand. I'm sorry I
mentioned it. Look, I'm just not in a position of
power there. Okay? Just forget it, okay? Just forget
it. It's no big thing.

MRS. MALLOY: Sorry I asked.

PHILIP MALLOY: It happened again.

MRS. MALLOY: What happened?

PHILIP MALLOY: In school. This morning. I was singing "The Star-Spangled Banner." The teacher kicked me out.

MR. MALLOY: You kidding?

PHILIP MALLOY: No, it's true.

MRS. MALLOY: Sent you out of the classroom?

PHILIP MALLOY: To the assistant principal's office.

MR. MALLOY: I hope you stood up for yourself.

PHILIP MALLOY: I spoke to Palleni.

MR. MALLOY: Who?

PHILIP MALLOY: Assistant principal.

MR. MALLOY: What did he say?

PHILIP MALLOY: Sided with Narwin.

MR. MALLOY: Phil, listen to me. Don't give in to that crap. Don't let them push you around. Singing the . . . There must be some mistake.

PHILIP MALLOY: That's the way she is.

MR. MALLOY: You have to stick up for yourself. That's all there is to it. Phil, do what you feel is right. We'll stand behind you.

MRS. MALLOY: It's so hard to believe.

PHILIP MALLOY: She's really nuts.

MR. MALLOY: Must be.

---

**9:45 P.M.**
**From a Letter Written by Margaret Narwin**
**to Her Sister, Anita Wigham**

---

. . . So you see, Anita, it was gratifying to hear Gertrude talk this way to me, exactly the kind of support teachers need. Certainly it's what I need at this time. I can't tell you how much. It bucks me up.

Many teachers have almost nothing good to say about their administrators, complaining that they fail to support them, much less grasp the complexities of the classroom situation, or that they show only slight concern about their problems. My principal is different.

I'm lucky. . . .

---

**11:05 P.M.**
**From the Diary of Philip Malloy**

---

Lots of kids bad-mouth their parents, say they never stick up for them or understand them. Or pay any attention to them. Stuff like that. My parents are different.

I'm lucky.

# Chapter 12

Friday, March 30

---

**8:05 A.M.**
**Discussion**
**in Margaret Narwin's Homeroom Class**

---

INTERCOM VOICE OF DR. GERTRUDE DOANE, HARRISON HIGH PRINCIPAL: Good morning to all students, faculty, and staff. Today is Friday, March 30. Today will be a Schedule B day.

Today in history: in 1746 on this date was the birth of Francisco José de Goya. In 1853 on this date Vincent van Gogh was born. In 1981, on this date, was the attempted assassination of President Ronald Reagan.

Please all rise and stand at respectful, silent attention for the playing of our national anthem.

*Oh, say, can you see by the dawn's early light . . .*

MISS NARWIN: Philip, is that you singing again?

*What so proudly we hailed at the twilight's last gleaming?*

*Whose broad stripes and bright stars, thro' the perilous fight . . .*

**MISS NARWIN:** Philip! I am talking to you!

**PHILIP MALLOY:** I have the right to do it.

*O'er the ramparts we watched were so gallantly streaming?*

*And the rockets' red glare, the bombs bursting in air . . .*

**MISS NARWIN:** The what?

**PHILIP MALLOY:** The right.

*Gave proof thro' the night that our flag was still there. . . .*

**MISS NARWIN:** I want you to stop it immediately. Your actions are thoroughly disrespectful.

**PHILIP MALLOY:** It's you who's being disrespectful!

*Oh, say does that star-spangled banner yet wave . . .*

**MISS NARWIN:** Philip!

*O'er the land of the free and the home of the brave?*

**PHILIP MALLOY:** I was being patriotic. That's all. It's a free country. You have no right to stop me. I was just singing to myself.

**MISS NARWIN:** Philip Malloy, you will leave this room immediately! Report to the principal's office.

**PHILIP MALLOY:** You can't keep me from being patriotic.

**MISS NARWIN:** Leave!

**PHILIP MALLOY:** I'm going. I'm going.

**DR. PALLENI:** Okay, Philip, you can come into the office. Go on, sit down. Didn't I just see you yesterday?

**PHILIP MALLOY:** Yeah.

**DR. PALLENI:** Something with you and Miss Narwin?

**PHILIP MALLOY:** Yeah.

**DR. PALLENI:** What's happened now?

**PHILIP MALLOY:** Nothing.

**DR. PALLENI:** Come on, Phil. Of course it's something. It may be unimportant. Or important. But it's *something.* Come on, look up at me. You can talk. Now, what's happening? What's going on?

**PHILIP MALLOY:** Miss Narwin . . .

**DR. PALLENI:** Go on.

**PHILIP MALLOY:** She won't let me sing "The Star-Spangled Banner."

**DR. PALLENI:** Isn't this what we were talking about the last time?

**PHILIP MALLOY:** She's against me being patriotic.

**DR. PALLENI:** I thought we agreed that when we have rules in schools, we stick with them. Didn't we agree to that?

**PHILIP MALLOY:** How can she keep me from singing the national anthem?

**DR. PALLENI:** Philip . . .

**PHILIP MALLOY:** Get me out of her classes.

**DR. PALLENI:** Look, Philip, what do you want me to do? Change the rules just for you? Do you?

**PHILIP MALLOY:** No, but . . .

**DR. PALLENI:** I had a real fistfight out there. Todd Becker. Arnie Lieber? You know them?

**PHILIP MALLOY:** Sort of.

**DR. PALLENI:** Serious fight. Todd took a licking. Ugly. Now, you come in here . . . Look, I'll be straight with you. This is your second time this week. Talk about rules, you're talking suspension. What do you say, Phil, you get up, go back there, and apologize? To Miss Narwin. Say you'll follow rules. Then, as far as I'm concerned, we forget it. Nothing on your record. What do you say?

**PHILIP MALLOY:** I was just singing. . . .

**DR. PALLENI:** Did you hear me?

**PHILIP MALLOY:** She's wrong. That's all. She's wrong. No way I'm apologizing.

**DR. PALLENI:** That's all you have to say?

**PHILIP MALLOY:** It's a free country.

**DR. PALLENI:** Nothing is free.

**PHILIP MALLOY:** Get me out of her classes.

**DR. PALLENI:** Phil, go sit out there for a while. Cool off. If you want to change your mind about this, tell Miss Mack out front you want to see me again. Otherwise—just so you understand—I check with Miss Narwin, and if she confirms what you said—

that you were breaking rules—hey, I call your folks, they come get you—boom!—two-day suspension. Get it? Automatic.

**PHILIP MALLOY:** But she's wrong.

**DR. PALLENI:** Philip, I'll level with you. You're the one who is wrong. You're here to get an education. Rules are rules. Now clear out. I've got important business here. Go on. Speak to Miss Mack out there if you change your mind.

**PHILIP MALLOY:** I'm not going to change my mind. We don't get along. Get me out of her classes.

**DR. PALLENI:** Philip, out!

---

**9:30 A.M.**
**Conversation between Dr. Joseph Palleni and Margaret Narwin**

---

**DR. PALLENI:** Excuse me, Miss Narwin, may I have a word with you?

**MISS NARWIN:** Class, just continue on with reading that scene. I'll be right outside.

**DR. PALLENI:** Sorry to bother you, Peg. Look, it's about this Phil Malloy.

**MISS NARWIN:** Something is certainly bothering that boy.

**DR. PALLENI:** Singing when you asked him not to.

**MISS NARWIN:** Quite provocative. Trying to create an incident.

**DR. PALLENI:** Any idea what it's about?

**MISS NARWIN:** No.

**DR. PALLENI:** I offered to get him out of this business by coming back and apologizing, but he won't. Two-day suspension.

**MISS NARWIN:** Maybe it would be better to switch him into another homeroom.

**DR. PALLENI:** That's what he suggested. And out of your English class too.

**MISS NARWIN:** He's been doing poorly there.

**DR. PALLENI:** Maybe that's it.

**MISS NARWIN:** I think he's lazy.

**DR. PALLENI:** Let's start with a homeroom change.

**MISS NARWIN:** He seems to get on with Bernie Lunser.

**DR. PALLENI:** Good idea.

**MISS NARWIN:** Suspension might be counterproductive.

**DR. PALLENI:** I hear you. Won't keep you. The parents might want to talk to you.

**MISS NARWIN:** I understand. I wish I could reach him. I just don't seem to. Really, a nice boy.

**DR. PALLENI:** Yeah. Good kid. Maybe something going on at home. Or hormones. Have a girlfriend?

**MISS NARWIN:** Joe, I wouldn't know.

**DR. PALLENI:** Okay, Peg. Sorry to bother you.

**MISS NARWIN:** Let me know if I can be of further help.

**DR. PALLENI:** Catch you later.

**DR. PALLENI:** Now, Philip, I checked with Miss Narwin, and she is in agreement with you. You did break the rules. She also made a point of saying she was prepared to let bygones be bygones if you do as I suggested, apologize and promise not to do that again.

**PHILIP MALLOY:** No.

**DR. PALLENI:** Hey, come on, Phil, it'll be a shame to put something down on your record. It's a perfectly good one.

**PHILIP MALLOY:** No.

**DR. PALLENI:** Then, Phil, I'm prepared to call one of your parents to come get you and take you home. You'll be out for the rest of the day and . . . I could make it Monday and Tuesday, but . . . How about just Monday? Give you a long weekend to think it out.

**PHILIP MALLOY:** I'm not going to change my mind.

**DR. PALLENI:** Okay, who do you want me to call? Your mother or your father?

**PHILIP MALLOY:** My father doesn't like to be called at work.

**DR. PALLENI:** Too bad. Is your mother reachable? I can't read a shrug.

**PHILIP MALLOY:** She works too.

DR. PALLENI: Where?

PHILIP MALLOY: At the phone company.

DR. PALLENI: I guess we can reach her. I'll call her. Last chance, Phil.

PHILIP MALLOY: Can't you just change—

DR. PALLENI: First things first. An apology.

PHILIP MALLOY: Call her.

---

**9:59 A.M.**
**Phone Conversation between**
**Dr. Joseph Palleni**
**and Mrs. Malloy**

---

DR. PALLENI: Hello? Is this Mrs. Malloy? Phil's mother?

MRS. MALLOY: Yes, it is.

DR. PALLENI: This is Dr. Palleni, assistant principal at Harrison High.

MRS. MALLOY: Is something the matter with Philip?

DR. PALLENI: Well, no, not exactly. He's sitting right here in front of me. In perfect health. Mrs. Malloy, I'm afraid we've had a little incident here—rule-breaking.

MRS. MALLOY: What happened?

DR. PALLENI: And breaking a rule twice in one week after he'd been warned once.

MRS. MALLOY: What rule?

DR. PALLENI: In fact, Philip was offered—I just offered it—a chance to apologize to the teacher in question, but he won't take it. So, I'm afraid—let me stress this is Phil's decision, not mine—what we have here is a two-day suspension situation. I'm afraid you'll have to come and take him home.

MRS. MALLOY: Now?

DR. PALLENI: Yes, now.

MRS. MALLOY: I'm at my job.

DR. PALLENI: I am sorry. You will have to come.

MRS. MALLOY: What rule did he break?

DR. PALLENI: We can talk about it when you get here. I'd rather we all—you, me, and Philip—talk about it together.

MRS. MALLOY: I have to get permission.

DR. PALLENI: I understand.

MRS. MALLOY: I'll come over.

DR. PALLENI: Thank you.

---

**10:04 A.M.**
**Conversation**
**between Philip Malloy**
**and Dr. Joseph Palleni**

---

PHILIP MALLOY: She coming?

DR. PALLENI: Did you think she wouldn't? Philip, you're bringing a bunch of grief to yourself. And a bother to her. Now, last chance—apologize?

PHILIP MALLOY: No.

DR. PALLENI: Go wait out there until your mother comes.

MR. MALLOY: Susan, I wish you wouldn't call me like this. It's very tense around here today.

MRS. MALLOY: I had to speak to you. I just got a call from Phil's school.

MR. MALLOY: Something the matter? What's up?

MRS. MALLOY: They're going to suspend him.

MR. MALLOY: Phil?

MRS. MALLOY: It was the principal. I have to go in and get him. He's suspended.

MR. MALLOY: Why?

MRS. MALLOY: Some rule.

MR. MALLOY: What rule? Didn't you ask?

MRS. MALLOY: They wouldn't tell me.

MR. MALLOY: They can't just . . .

MRS. MALLOY: I'm really upset.

MR. MALLOY: What it is, is they're really after the kid.

MRS. MALLOY: I don't know. . . .

MR. MALLOY: I'm going to give them a piece of my mind.

MRS. MALLOY: Don't you think we should—

MR. MALLOY: Susan, the kid has done nothing!

MRS. MALLOY: We can speak—

MR. MALLOY: Honey, I have to go. Something just came up.

**10:10 A.M.**

## MEMO

### HARRISON SCHOOL DISTRICT

Where Our Children Are Educated,
Not Just Taught

Dr. Albert Seymour  Mrs. Gloria Harland
*Superintendent* *Chairman, School Board*

TO: PHILIP MALLOY
FROM: DR. JOSEPH PALLENI,
    ASSISTANT PRINCIPAL,
    HARRISON HIGH SCHOOL
RE: NEW HOMEROOM ASSIGNMENTS
    FOR SPRING TERM

Dear <u>Philip   </u>,
   As we head into the Spring term, the faculty committee has made some changes in homeroom assignments. This will facilitate the movements of students, as well as allow for a greater degree of freedom in the planning of Spring term extracurricular schedules.
   Your new homeroom teacher is: <u>Mr. Lunser</u> in room: <u>304.</u> Effective <u>Tuesday, April 3, 8 A.M.</u>
   Thank you for your cooperation.

Dr. Joseph Palleni
*Assistant Principal*

DR. PALLENI: Okay, this is what we've got here. Philip broke a rule. Twice. He and I talked it over earlier this week. I made it clear what would happen. We try to be flexible, but we still have rules. Everybody has to work together. Cooperation. If a student creates a disturbance in a classroom, that's breaking a rule. An important rule. Students cannot break—cannot make a disturbance in a classroom. Straightforward rule infraction. Now, we offered Philip here a chance—he has a perfectly clean record—an opportunity to apologize to the teacher in question. I'll offer it again. Will you do that, Phil, apologize, so we can just end all this?

PHILIP MALLOY: She really dislikes me.

DR. PALLENI: Who is that?

PHILIP MALLOY: Not will.

MRS. MALLOY: Philip has been saying that—

DR. PALLENI: Look, Mrs. Malloy, I don't want to get into that. Philip admits he broke a rule.

MRS. MALLOY: What rule?

DR. PALLENI: Disturbing a class.

PHILIP MALLOY: Singing the national anthem.

MRS. MALLOY: Is that the rule?

DR. PALLENI: Yes, disturbing the class.

MRS. MALLOY: I just can't believe that—

DR. PALLENI: Excuse me. Philip, did you break the rule?

PHILIP MALLOY: It's a dumb rule.

DR. PALLENI: See? He's admitting it. Mrs. Malloy, it is my job—one of my jobs—to make sure the school— the kids, the staff, the teachers—works together in harmony. I'm sure we agree that we can't have kids deciding which rules to follow and which rules not to follow. I really don't wish to discuss it. Two-day suspension. For the rest of today. And Monday. Be back on Tuesday.

MRS. MALLOY: I just want to say I don't think it's right. I mean, singing the—

DR. PALLENI: Excuse me. Are you saying that kids should only follow the rules they want to?

MRS. MALLOY: No, but—

DR. PALLENI: Then we're in agreement. Thank you for coming in. Philip, I hope you think about it.

---

**11:02 A.M.**
**Conversation**
**between Philip Malloy and His Mother**
**on Their Way Home**

---

MRS. MALLOY: Phil, what *is* this all about?

PHILIP MALLOY: I told you, that teacher . . .

MRS. MALLOY: You've never been suspended.

PHILIP MALLOY: It's her.

MRS. MALLOY: But why?

PHILIP MALLOY: I don't know.

MRS. MALLOY: They said you could apologize.

PHILIP MALLOY: Nothing to apologize about.

MRS. MALLOY: Your father is going to be very upset.

PHILIP MALLOY: Yeah, well, he told me I should stick up for myself. Said I shouldn't let her push me around. That she was wrong and I was right. So I did.

MRS. MALLOY: When did he say that?

PHILIP MALLOY: Last night. Said I should do what was right.

MRS. MALLOY: Mr.—What's his name?

PHILIP MALLOY: Palleni.

MRS. MALLOY: —said you were creating a disturbance.

PHILIP MALLOY: Bull. It's all her fault.

MRS. MALLOY: Who?

PHILIP MALLOY: Narwin!

MRS. MALLOY: We'll talk it out with your father when he gets home tonight.

PHILIP MALLOY: No way I'm going back to her class again.

MRS. MALLOY: Sometimes I think we should have sent you to Washington Academy.

PHILIP MALLOY: Geeky private school? No way.

MRS. MALLOY: We'll talk. I just want you to know I'm very upset.

PHILIP MALLOY: Sorry.

# MEMO

## HARRISON SCHOOL DISTRICT

Where Our Children Are Educated,
Not Just Taught

Dr. Albert Seymour  Mrs. Gloria Harland
*Superintendent* *Chairman, School Board*

TO: MARGARET NARWIN
FROM: DR. JOSEPH PALLENI,
    ASSISTANT PRINCIPAL,
    HARRISON HIGH SCHOOL
RE: PHILIP MALLOY

Philip Malloy has been suspended for two days—effective today—for causing a disturbance in your homeroom class. I also transferred him back to Mr. Lunser for homeroom.

## MEMO

### HARRISON SCHOOL DISTRICT

Where Our Children Are Educated,
Not Just Taught

Dr. Albert Seymour  Mrs. Gloria Harland
*Superintendent* *Chairman, School Board*

TO: BERNARD LUNSER
FROM: DR. JOSEPH PALLENI,
      ASSISTANT PRINCIPAL,
      HARRISON HIGH SCHOOL
RE: PHILIP MALLOY

Philip Malloy will be returning to you as his homeroom teacher effective April 3. He has been suspended for two days—effective today—for causing a disturbance in Miss Narwin's class. While what is involved here is only a minor infraction, more acting out than anything else, there may be some personal problems with the boy (at home?), so I would appreciate hearing from you as to Philip's behavior in your class. I should like to be helpful to him.

## MEMO

---

### HARRISON SCHOOL DISTRICT

Where Our Children Are Educated,
Not Just Taught

Dr. Albert Seymour  Mrs. Gloria Harland
*Superintendent* *Chairman, School Board*

TO: DR. GERTRUDE DOANE, PRINCIPAL
FROM: DR. JOSEPH PALLENI,
   ASSISTANT PRINCIPAL,
   HARRISON HIGH SCHOOL
RE: PHILIP MALLOY

Philip Malloy (ninth grade) has been suspended for two days—effective today—for causing a disturbance in Miss Narwin's homeroom class. Because I feel that the problem may have arisen out of some obscure tension between teacher and student, I decided it was advisable to transfer the boy to Mr. Lunser's homeroom.

Since I assume nothing more will come of this, I'm not aware of anything here that requires your further attention.

DR. PALLENI: Oh, Peg! I know you're rushing off. Look, just want you to know I took care of the Malloy boy. Talked to his mother. She understands. Couple of days' suspension. No big deal.

MISS NARWIN: Did you have to suspend him?

DR. PALLENI: The rule. Two infractions in one week. Anyway, I put a memo in your box. Also, switched him back to Bernie for homeroom. What about his English class?

MISS NARWIN: I don't want to give up on him yet.

DR. PALLENI: Whatever you say

MISS NARWIN: He's really a nice boy. Thanks for taking care of it.

DR. PALLENI: No problem.

MISS NARWIN: I have a class. . . .

DR. PALLENI: Have a good one.

KEN BARCHET: Hey, Phil, what's happening?

PHILIP MALLOY: Nothing. Going out to deliver my papers.

**KEN BARCHET:** I heard you got suspended.

**PHILIP MALLOY:** Yeah.

**KEN BARCHET:** For how long?

**PHILIP MALLOY:** Couple of days.

**KEN BARCHET:** What for?

**PHILIP MALLOY:** You were there.

**KEN BARCHET:** Because of your singing?

**PHILIP MALLOY:** Yeah.

**KEN BARCHET:** I thought that was funny. Too cool.

**PHILIP MALLOY:** Wasn't loud.

**KEN BARCHET:** I heard it. She'd like to throw a fit.

**PHILIP MALLOY:** Yeah.

**KEN BARCHET:** I mean, far-out. What made you do it?

**PHILIP MALLOY:** Free country.

**KEN BARCHET:** Not as if you have a good voice. People were cracking up.

**PHILIP MALLOY:** I know. Was Allison laughing?

**KEN BARCHET:** I don't know. We going to work out after your deliveries?

**PHILIP MALLOY:** Sure.

**KEN BARCHET:** See you at the park.

ALLISON DORESETT: Is this Phil?

PHILIP MALLOY: Yeah.

ALLISON DORESETT: This is Allison.

PHILIP MALLOY: Oh, hi.

ALLISON DORESETT: Is it true that you got suspended?

PHILIP MALLOY: Yeah.

ALLISON DORESETT: Why?

PHILIP MALLOY: Nothing. You were there.

ALLISON DORESETT: The singing?

PHILIP MALLOY: Yeah. "The Star-Spangled Banner."

ALLISON DORESETT: That?

PHILIP MALLOY: Yeah. Narwin got me kicked out.

ALLISON DORESETT: You're kidding. She wouldn't do that.

PHILIP MALLOY: She did. You saw it.

ALLISON DORESETT: No, I mean, she's nice.

PHILIP MALLOY: I don't think so.

ALLISON DORESETT: For how long?

PHILIP MALLOY: Two days.

ALLISON DORESETT: Wow. You must have really got on her
nerves.

PHILIP MALLOY: Just singing . . . humming.

ALLISON DORESETT: Well, I just wanted to know. People were talking.

PHILIP MALLOY: What were they saying?

ALLISON DORESETT: You know. How weird. See you.

PHILIP MALLOY: See you.

---

**5:30 P.M.**
**From a Letter Written by Margaret Narwin to Her Sister, Anita Wigham**

---

. . . So you see, Anita, what intrigues me about this new concept of teaching English—Whole Language — is that it has its focus on *literature,* and in a way that I think young people will find very interesting. Still, I can hear you say, "It's just another education fad."

You may be right. But if the truth be known, Anita, teaching is exhausting. And what I say is this: if it takes a "fad" to pump energy back into the classroom, why, it's worth it just for that!

Sorry to have gone on so long about this. It's just caught my fancy. I can hardly think about anything else.

Oh, yes, do you remember my writing to you about a student I have, Philip Malloy? I'm convinced now that there is something going on in this boy's private life that is deeply troubling to him. Twice this week I had to send him out for being disruptive in a singularly disrespectful way. Our society is always asking schools to do what is not done at home. Then Joe Palleni (assistant principal) felt compelled to suspend him for a bit, something I *never* believe is productive. I told him that too. In fact, Philip is a nice boy. So I do feel badly about the whole thing. I always do when I lose a student. Next week—-when he comes back—I intend to sit down with him and have a heart-to-heart talk.

This weekend I'll be visiting with Barbara Benthave. She and her husband . . .

---

**6:45 P.M.**
**Discussion**
**between Philip Malloy's Parents**

---

MRS. MALLOY: Oh, hi, honey.

MR. MALLOY: Where's Philip?

MRS. MALLOY: Up in the shower. Just got back from running.

MR. MALLOY: You talk to him about what happened?

MRS. MALLOY: When I drove him home. But I had to get right back to work. It's just what I told you. How was your day?

MR. MALLOY: Rotten. Dexter is still sore at me.

MRS. MALLOY: Get yourself a drink to settle down first. We have plenty of time to talk over dinner.

MR. MALLOY: Sure.

---

**7:12 P.M.**
**Discussion**
**between Philip Malloy and His Parents**
**During Dinner**

---

MR. MALLOY: Okay, Phil. Now, I want to hear the whole thing. Start to finish. Just understand, right from the start, we're on your side. We don't intend to just take it. But I have to know what happened. Go on now.

**PHILIP MALLOY:** Same as before.

**MR. MALLOY:** Same as *what* before?

**MRS. MALLOY:** He's trying to tell you, dear.

**PHILIP MALLOY:** See, they play "The Star-Spangled Banner" at the beginning of school. . . .

**MR. MALLOY:** I understand. When I was a kid we pledged allegiance. Go on.

**PHILIP MALLOY:** A tape.

**MR. MALLOY:** Okay.

**PHILIP MALLOY:** When—before—when I was in Mr. Lunser's class, he was like, almost asking me to sing out loud.

**MRS. MALLOY:** I always thought Philip had a good voice.

**MR. MALLOY:** That's not exactly relevant! Go on.

**PHILIP MALLOY:** But this teacher—

**MR. MALLOY:** Mrs. Narwin.

**PHILIP MALLOY:** It's Miss.

**MR. MALLOY:** Figures.

**MRS. MALLOY:** That has nothing to do with it, Ben!

**MR. MALLOY:** Go on.

**PHILIP MALLOY:** She won't let me. Threw me out of class.

**MRS. MALLOY:** The principal said it was a rule.

**PHILIP MALLOY:** Ma, he's the *assistant* principal.

MR. MALLOY: But why does this mean suspension?

PHILIP MALLOY: She threw me out twice this week.

MR. MALLOY: It seems arbitrary. Outrageous.

MRS. MALLOY: Stupid rules.

MR. MALLOY: Right. How can you have a rule against singing "The Star-Spangled Banner"?

PHILIP MALLOY: Ask Narwin.

MR. MALLOY: You know who I bet would be interested in this?

PHILIP MALLOY: Who?

MR. MALLOY: Ted Griffen.

MRS. MALLOY: Why?

MR. MALLOY: He's a neighbor. A friend. And he's running for school board. He should be interested. That's what the board does. Keeps the schools in line.

PHILIP MALLOY: He won't be able to do anything. If I could just get out of her classes.

MR. MALLOY: Maybe. Maybe not. Phil, we intend to support you on this.

---

**8:40 P.M.
Conversation
among Philip Malloy, Mr. Malloy,
and Ted Griffen**

---

PHILIP MALLOY: Dad, I don't think he'll be interested.

MR. MALLOY: Of course he will. Now, just let me do the talking. Ted! Hello.

**MR. GRIFFEN:** Oh, Ben. Hello. Is that you, Philip? How you guys doing?

**MR. MALLOY:** Ted, got a minute? This a bad time?

**MR. GRIFFEN:** Well, I am in the middle of a talk with— why, what's up?

**MR. MALLOY:** Something about school. And Phil here. . . .

**MR. GRIFFEN:** I'm not on the school board yet, Ben. Trying, but not yet.

**MR. MALLOY:** That's the point. This is something that happened to Phil at school.

**MR. GRIFFEN:** I don't know if I should . . .

**MR. MALLOY:** He was suspended for *singing* "The Star-Spangled Banner."

**MR. GRIFFEN:** What?

**MR. MALLOY:** You heard me. Phil was kicked out of school for singing "The Star-Spangled Banner."

**MR. GRIFFEN:** Are you serious?

**MR. MALLOY:** I know. It's crazy. Today.

**MR. GRIFFEN:** That true?

**PHILIP MALLOY:** Yes, sir.

**MR. GRIFFEN:** Singing?

**MR. MALLOY:** We couldn't believe it at first either. But they called Susan at work, mind you. Made her leave work and bring him home. Two-day suspension. For *singing*.

**MR. GRIFFEN:** Who did it?

**MR. MALLOY:** The principal.

PHILIP MALLOY: Assistant principal.

MR. GRIFFEN: When were you singing?

MR. MALLOY: Tell him.

PHILIP MALLOY: They sing, play the . . . the national anthem in the morning. And I, like—I was singing it. Mostly to myself. Then, I have this teacher—people don't like her—and she, well, she threw me out of the class and—

MR. GRIFFEN: Wait a minute. I want to get this straight. Look, I have this reporter I'm talking to. Jennifer Stewart. From the *Manchester Record*. School beat. How about talking to me with her there?

MR. MALLOY: What do you say?

PHILIP MALLOY: A reporter?

MR. GRIFFEN: She does their educational stuff. She's covering school board elections around the state. A good person.

PHILIP MALLOY: I don't know. . . .

MR. GRIFFEN: Nothing to worry about. Very straightforward. I'd like her to hear about this. Really, I would. Just tell her the truth. You don't mind, do you, Ben?

MR. MALLOY: No.

MR. GRIFFEN: Phil?

PHILIP MALLOY: Well . . .

MR. GRIFFEN: Sure. Just tell her the truth. Come on in.

8:45 P.M.
Conversation among
Philip Malloy, Mr. Malloy, Ted Griffen,
and Jennifer Stewart,
Education Reporter
from the *Manchester Record*

**MR. GRIFFEN:** Jennifer, this is my neighbor from across the street, Ben Malloy. His son, Phil Malloy. Jennifer Stewart, from the *Manchester Record*.

**MS. STEWART:** Pleased to meet you.

**MR. MALLOY:** Evening.

**MR. GRIFFEN:** Jennifer was just interviewing me for a piece she's doing on the school board elections. Statewide. These guys think I'm such a shoo-in to be elected they're already bringing me problems.

**MS. STEWART:** Shows a lot of confidence in you.

**MR. GRIFFEN:** Actually, people are tired of the old ways. Not happy with the way things are. Now, for example, this thing, these guys, Phil here, tells me something that's outrageous. Something I would never condone.

**MS. STEWART:** What's that?

**MR. MALLOY:** Phil, tell her what you told Ted.

**MS. STEWART:** This something . . . Is it Philip?

**MR. MALLOY:** Yes. Philip. M—a—l—l—o—y.

**MS. STEWART:** This something that happened to you?

**MR. GRIFFEN:** He lives right across the street. Neighbors. Old—and good—friends.

**MR. MALLOY:** Phil, tell her what happened. Exactly as it was. This was just today.

**MS. STEWART:** Philip?

**PHILIP MALLOY:** Well, see, there's this teacher.

**MR. MALLOY:** Go on.

**PHILIP MALLOY:** Miss Narwin, English teacher, and she doesn't like me. . . .

**MR. GRIFFEN:** No. Tell her what you told me.

**MR. MALLOY:** This is part of it.

**MS. STEWART:** Tell it your own way, Philip.

**PHILIP MALLOY:** In the mornings, at school, in homeroom, before morning announcements, they play "The Star-Spangled Banner."

**MS. STEWART:** Who plays?

**PHILIP MALLOY:** The school. On the sound system.

**MS. STEWART:** Just want to get this down. Okay. Go on.

**PHILIP MALLOY:** And, I like to sing along.

**MR. MALLOY:** It's the way we've brought him up.

**MR. GRIFFEN:** The whole neighborhood is like that.

**MS. STEWART:** Go on, Philip.

**PHILIP MALLOY:** And this teacher . . .

**MS. STEWART:** Could you spell her name?

**PHILIP MALLOY:** Miss Narwin.

**MR. MALLOY:** M—a—r—w—i—n. She's always on the boy's back. Bad teacher. The kids don't like her.

**MR. GRIFFEN:** Narwin? Or Marwin?

**MR. MALLOY:** Right.

**MS. STEWART:** Go on, Philip.

**PHILIP MALLOY:** Well, I like to, you know, sing along. But, see, she kicked me out. For singing it.

**MS. STEWART:** The national anthem?

**MR. GRIFFEN:** Hard to believe.

**MR. MALLOY:** It's true. The principal even admitted it to my wife.

**PHILIP MALLOY:** Assistant principal.

**MR. MALLOY:** Well, anyway, they admit it.

**MS. STEWART:** Is there more?

**PHILIP MALLOY:** It happened again.

**MS. STEWART:** Twice?

**PHILIP MALLOY:** Yeah. Three times, actually.

**MS. STEWART:** And?

**PHILIP MALLOY:** They suspended me.

**MR. GRIFFEN:** How anyone could get kicked out of school for . . .

**MR. MALLOY:** Being patriotic.

**MR. GRIFFEN:** If I were on the board, I wouldn't accept this. I could not condone this. No way.

**MS. STEWART:** Philip, was anyone else kicked out?

**PHILIP MALLOY:** Just me.

**MS. STEWART:** Do you have any sense as to why you in particular?

**PHILIP MALLOY:** They have a rule against it.

**MS. STEWART:** Rule against what?

**MR. MALLOY:** Singing "The Star-Spangled Banner."

**MR. GRIFFEN:** Absurd!

**MS. STEWART:** And this is something I can check out?

**PHILIP MALLOY:** I guess. Sure. Go on.

**MR. MALLOY:** The principal admitted it.

**MR. GRIFFEN:** Jennifer, and you can quote me on this, I don't intend to be silent about this issue. This is a school, an American school, and parents have a right to expect that certain things, like values, will be taught. Community values. Things I believe in. I mean that. Sincerely.

---

**11:34 P.M.**
**From the Diary of Philip Malloy**

---

It really hit the fan today. So much happened I have a headache. It's going to take a while to think out. Actually, I don't feel so great. In a way, the whole thing is stupid. But everybody says I was right. And I was.

# Chapter 13

Saturday, March 31

**10:00 A.M.**
**Phone Conversation**
**between Jennifer Stewart of the**
***Manchester Record***
**and Dr. Albert Seymour,**
**Harrison School Superintendent**

**MS. STEWART:** May I speak to Dr. Albert Seymour, please.

**DR. SEYMOUR:** Speaking.

**MS. STEWART:** Dr. Seymour, this is Jennifer Stewart of the *Manchester Record.*

**DR. SEYMOUR:** How do you do?

**MS. STEWART:** I hope you don't mind a call at home. I'm the education reporter.

**DR. SEYMOUR:** Oh, yes.

**MS. STEWART:** Something has come up—a report, sir— and I wanted to check some facts with you.

**DR. SEYMOUR:** If I can be helpful . . . certainly.

**MS. STEWART:** Sir, does the Harrison School District have a rule that forbids students from singing "The Star-Spangled Banner"?

**DR. SEYMOUR:** Beg pardon?

**MS. STEWART:** Yes, sir. Does the Harrison School District have a rule that students are not allowed to sing "The Star-Spangled Banner"?

**DR. SEYMOUR:** Of course not. Whatever gave you that idea? Who told you that?

**MS. STEWART:** There's been a claim . . .

**DR. SEYMOUR:** Hogwash. You should check your sources.

**MS. STEWART:** I'm checking them right now.

**DR. SEYMOUR:** The answer is no. We do not have such a rule. Absolutely.

**MS. STEWART:** May I quote you?

**DR. SEYMOUR:** Of course.

**MS. STEWART:** Thank you.

**DR. SEYMOUR:** You're quite welcome.

---

**10:15 A.M.**
**Phone Conversation**
**between Jennifer Stewart**
**of the *Manchester Record***
**and Dr. Gertrude Doane,**
**Principal, Harrison High**

---

**MS. STEWART:** May I speak to Dr. Doane, please.

**DR. DOANE:** This is she.

**MS. STEWART:** Dr. Doane, my name is Jennifer Stewart, of the *Manchester Record*. I do the school stories. Sorry to bother you on a Saturday. . . .

**DR. DOANE:** Yes?

**MS. STEWART:** I'm checking out an item that's come to our attention. It would appear that one of your students, Philip Malloy—

**DR. DOANE:** Ninth grade.

**MS. STEWART:** You know him?

**DR. DOANE:** Oh, yes. Nice boy. Know him well. Has something happened to him?

**MS. STEWART:** This is in reference to his suspension from school.

**DR. DOANE:** Suspension?

**MS. STEWART:** Isn't that something—a suspension—that as principal you would know something about?

**DR. DOANE:** Well, yes. . . .

**MS. STEWART:** On Friday, March 30, yesterday, Philip Malloy—*he* claims, as his parents claim, that he was suspended from your high school for two days.

**DR. DOANE:** Discipline problems are usually in the hands of my assistant principal, Dr. Palleni. In any case I was at meetings all—

**MS. STEWART:** Wouldn't Dr. Palleni discuss such a suspension with you first?

**DR. DOANE:** That would depend on . . . Ms. . . .

**MS. STEWART:** Stewart.

DR. DOANE: Ms. Stewart, actually I'm not sure I should be discussing this matter with you. Records regarding our children are of a confidential nature.

MS. STEWART: It's already a matter of public record. The boy—and his father—have made a public statement. They claim he was suspended.

DR. DOANE: That's what you say.

MS. STEWART: Dr. Doane, if you don't wish to cooperate . . .

DR. DOANE: Now just one moment, Ms. . . .

MS. STEWART: Stewart.

DR. DOANE: Ms. Stewart, you call me up and inform me about something of which I have had no prior information. . . .

MS. STEWART: Then you didn't know about this?

DR. DOANE: I just said—

MS. STEWART: Ms. Doane—

DR. DOANE: *Dr.* Doane.

MS. STEWART: Excuse me. Dr. Doane, Philip Malloy, who is a student at your school, and who you claim to know well, has made a statement to the effect that he was suspended for singing "The Star-Spangled Banner."

DR. DOANE: Oh, really!

MS. STEWART: His father claims this is true. Now, I just spoke to your superintendent. . . .

DR. DOANE: Dr. Seymour?

**MS. STEWART:** That's right. And he says that the Harrison School District has no such rule. So, I am just trying to sort this out. . . .

**DR. DOANE:** I don't know the particulars of this situation. You've only just informed me about it. I see no reason to be talking to a reporter about a student's problem. In any case, it doesn't seem to have happened. The superintendent told you we have no such rule.

**MS. STEWART:** Would a student in your school run into difficulty by singing the national anthem?

**DR. DOANE:** Of course not. But I repeat: discipline problems of a minor nature are handled by my assistant principal.

**MS. STEWART:** Palleni?

**DR. DOANE:** That's right. Dr. Joseph Palleni.

**MS. STEWART:** Thank you.

---

**10:30 A.M.**
**Discussion**
**between Philip Malloy and His Mother**

---

**PHILIP MALLOY:** Hey, Ma, look! Look at this letter.

**MRS. MALLOY:** What letter?

**PHILIP MALLOY:** Just came in the mail. Look. They shifted me out of Narwin's homeroom class. Back to Mr. Lunser.

**MRS. MALLOY:** Let me see. Well, that's something. They must have seen something was wrong there. Maybe you can go back to school Monday.

**PHILIP MALLOY:** Says it won't happen till Tuesday. When I go back.

**MRS. MALLOY:** May be just as well. I don't want you to have to deal with that woman again.

**PHILIP MALLOY:** But I still have her for English.

**MRS. MALLOY:** Didn't they change that?

**PHILIP MALLOY:** No.

**MRS. MALLOY:** But if they admit they're wrong about the one thing . . .

**PHILIP MALLOY:** Bet they just forgot to say that. Where's Dad?

**MRS. MALLOY:** Went to the store. Feel better?

**PHILIP MALLOY:** Yeah. But the English . . .

**MRS. MALLOY:** You just said they forgot.

**PHILIP MALLOY:** I guess. . . .

---

**10:40 A.M.**
**Phone Conversation**
**between Jennifer Stewart**
**of the *Manchester Record***
**and Dr. and Mrs. Joseph Palleni**

---

**MS. STEWART:** May I speak to Dr. Joseph Palleni, please?

**MRS. PALLENI:** Who's calling, please?

**MS. STEWART:** Jennifer Stewart, reporter for the *Manchester Record*.

**MRS. PALLENI:** He's in the backyard. I'll get him.

**MS. STEWART:** Appreciate that.

**DR. PALLENI:** Hello? This is Dr. Palleni.

**MS. STEWART:** Dr. Palleni, this is Jennifer Stewart. I'm a reporter for the *Manchester Record*. I'm doing a story—I've already spoken with your superintendent, Dr. Seymour, and your principal, Dr. Doane—

**DR. PALLENI:** What is this about?

**MS. STEWART:** Dr. Palleni, according to Dr. Seymour, the Harrison School District has no rule that would keep a student from singing "The Star-Spangled Banner."

**DR. PALLENI:** Did you say *singing?*

**MS. STEWART:** Yes. Is that your understanding?

**DR. PALLENI:** Well . . .

**MS. STEWART:** Now your principal, Dr. Doane, says that you are in charge of discipline in the school.

**DR. PALLENI:** *With* her.

**MS. STEWART:** With her?

**DR. PALLENI:** I always keep her informed.

**MS. STEWART:** Did you inform her that on Friday you suspended a student, Philip Malloy, for singing "The Star-Spangled Banner"?

**DR. PALLENI:** I did no such thing!

**MS. STEWART:** You didn't inform your superior, or you didn't suspend the boy for singing "The Star-Spangled Banner"? Which? I am simply trying to get my facts straight. Dr. Palleni? Are you still there?

**DR. PALLENI:** I don't wish to talk to you.

**MS. STEWART:** No comment?

**DR. PALLENI:** No comment. But you've got your facts all wrong.

**MS. STEWART:** Is that your comment?

**DR. PALLENI:** No comment.

**MS. STEWART:** I'm sorry. Should I call you back?

**DR. PALLENI:** Not to talk about this.

**MS. STEWART:** May I quote you?

**DR. PALLENI:** Thank you. Good-bye.

---

**11:00 A.M.**
**Phone Conversation**
**between Jennifer Stewart**
**of the *Manchester Record***
**and Margaret Narwin**

---

**MS. STEWART:** Margaret Narwin, please.

**MISS NARWIN:** Speaking.

**MS. STEWART:** Miss Narwin, my name is Jennifer Stewart, of the *Manchester Record*. The education reporter. I'm trying to write a story regarding an incident—something that appears to have happened in your school, in your class. I understand you are a teacher.

**MISS NARWIN:** An English teacher. In the high school.

**MS. STEWART:** How long have you taught there?

**MISS NARWIN:** For twenty-one years. What incident are you referring to? I'm not aware . . .

**MS. STEWART:** I'm simply trying to get the facts correct. Wanting to be fair to all concerned. I'm sure you can appreciate that.

**MISS NARWIN:** Are you sure this has something to do with me?

**MS. STEWART:** That appears to be the case. And, as I say, I want to be fair to all concerned, and report the facts correctly.

**MISS NARWIN:** I'm afraid I don't understand. . . .

**MS. STEWART:** I spoke to your superintendent, your principal, and your assistant principal, as well as Philip Malloy and his father.

**MISS NARWIN:** Who?

**MS. STEWART:** Philip Malloy. I believe he is one of your students.

**MISS NARWIN:** Well . . .

**MS. STEWART:** Now, as I understand it, the boy was dismissed from your class, then suspended from school because—he says it's a question of patriotism with him—he sang "The Star-Spangled Banner" during opening exercises in school in your class. Could you shed some light on this? Miss Narwin? Are you there?

**MISS NARWIN:** Yes. . . .

**MS. STEWART:** Could you give me your side of the story?

**MISS NARWIN:** The boy was creating a disturbance.

**MS. STEWART:** I'm sorry. I couldn't hear you. Could you speak up?

**MISS NARWIN:** The boy was creating a serious disturbance.

MS. STEWART: By singing the national anthem?

MISS NARWIN: We have a rule. . . .

MS. STEWART: Your superintendent, Dr. Seymour, says there is no rule.

MISS NARWIN: I don't think I should be talking about this.

MS. STEWART: But you do acknowledge that you sent him from your room?

MISS NARWIN: Yes, but . . .

MS. STEWART: For singing our national anthem?

MISS NARWIN: I think you need to speak to our principal.

MS. STEWART: I did speak to her.

MISS NARWIN: Then I have nothing more to say.

MS. STEWART: You are sure?

MISS NARWIN: Quite sure.

MS. STEWART: Thank you, Miss . . . or is it *Mrs.* Narwin?

MISS NARWIN: Miss.

MS. STEWART: Thank you.

MISS NARWIN: Thank you.

---

**11:15 A.M.**
**Phone Conversation**
**between Dr. Gertrude Doane**
**and Dr. Joseph Palleni**

---

DR. DOANE: Joe, sorry to bother you at home.

DR. PALLENI: That's all right. . . .

**DR. DOANE:** I just got a call from a newspaper reporter— *Manchester Record—*

**DR. PALLENI:** Oh, right. She called me.

**DR. DOANE:** She did?

**DR. PALLENI:** About a suspension—Philip Malloy. On Friday.

**DR. DOANE:** What is this? I was at district meetings. What's this all about? Why should a reporter be calling?

**DR. PALLENI:** I put a memo in your box. Yesterday.

**DR. DOANE:** Joe, I was at meetings.

**DR. PALLENI:** Right. I know. Okay. The Malloy boy was suspended for two days—actually, less—because he was causing a disturbance in Peg Narwin's class.

**DR. DOANE:** Joe, what this reporter said—told me—it was for *singing* "The Star-Spangled Banner." What's this all about?

**DR. PALLENI:** Oh, no, no. Nothing like that. It was just that he—Philip—was acting out in class. Look, Gert, he did it twice this week. So I had to suspend him. Look. I, you know, I talked it over with the kid. He agrees about what happened. He does. That's not an issue. Besides, I gave him a chance to work it out, you know, apologize, promise not to do it again. He's okay. I mean, his record is perfect. Didn't seem like much of a thing. But he wouldn't swallow his pride. Something else, I suspect. At home. Hormones. You name it. Anyway, that's all it is.

**DR. DOANE:** But why should a reporter call me?

DR. PALLENI: I don't know. As I said, she called me too.

DR. DOANE: What did you tell her?

DR. PALLENI: Told her to mind her own business.

DR. DOANE: Joe . . .

DR. PALLENI: Good Lord, Gert, if I had to discuss every little problem we have with the kids with every fool reporter . . .

DR. DOANE: I know. I know.

DR. PALLENI: Do you want me to talk to her? Suppose I could track her down.

DR. DOANE: Not if it was only what you said it was.

DR. PALLENI: It was. Believe me. It was.

DR. DOANE: Okay. If she does call back, you can just refer her to me.

DR. PALLENI: Will do.

DR. DOANE: Have a nice weekend, Joe. Sorry to bother you.

DR. PALLENI: No problem. Have a good one, Gert.

---

### 11:45 P.M.
### From the Diary of Philip Malloy

---

Aside from getting out of Narwin's homeroom—still not out of her English—not much of anything today. Boring! Newspapers to deliver. Collection day. Can't understand how people who want the paper think they can get away with not paying for it. And it comes out of my pocket. Then folks made me do yard work. Clean up room. Ken came over.

Been trying to figure a way to get on the school track team. Maybe—like the coach said—I should ask Narwin for extra work. Be worth it. I hate working out without a team. . . .

# Chapter 14

Sunday, April 1

---

**Article
from the Community Section of
the *Manchester Record***

---

SUSPENDED FOR PATRIOTISM
by J. Stewart, Education Reporter

*Harrison.* While it may appear to be an April Fools' Day joke, tenth grader Philip Malloy of Harrison High School was suspended for singing "The Star-Spangled Banner."

His parents, Susan and Benjamin Malloy of Harrison Township, do not consider themselves super-patriots, but they did raise their son to have pride in our country. It was only natural then for Philip to sing along when the national anthem was played on tape during morning exercises. According to Harrison School superintendent Dr. A. Seymour, there is no rule against singing the anthem. Indeed, in every other class Philip did just that. His new homeroom teacher, Ms. Margaret Narwin, however, changed the rules. Every time Philip lifted his voice to sing she threw him out of class, insisting a disturbance was being created.

School principal Dr. Gertrude Doane, who admits that Philip has no previous bad marks on his record, saw the issue only as one of discipline, and referred all questions regarding school policy to Dr. Joseph Palleni, assistant principal. Dr. Palleni, however, refused to be interviewed regarding the incident.

What will young Malloy—who has his own delivery route for the *Manchester Record*—do during his suspension from school? Philip, who still hopes to make the school track team this spring, said, "Try to keep up with my work, and work out with classmates after school."

Harrison Township will be voting on a new school district budget this spring, along with a new school board.

---

**8:30 A.M.**
**Phone Conversation**
**between Dr. Albert Seymour**
**and Dr. Gertrude Doane**

---

**DR. SEYMOUR:** Gertrude?

**DR. DOANE:** This is Gertrude Doane.

**DR. SEYMOUR:** Gertrude, Al Seymour here. Did you see this morning's paper?

**DR. DOANE:** Just reading the first section now.

**DR. SEYMOUR:** Well, look at section D. Community news. Page two. School news.

**DR. DOANE:** Why?

**DR. SEYMOUR:** Just do it.

DR. DOANE: Hold on a moment.

DR. SEYMOUR: Did you find it?

DR. DOANE: Yes, and I . . . Oh my!

DR. SEYMOUR: Read it.

DR. DOANE: This is ridiculous!

DR. SEYMOUR: What is this business? I had a call from a reporter yesterday, but . . . Is any of this true?

DR. DOANE: Al, the boy was not suspended because of singing the national anthem. Of course not. He was suspended because he was creating a disturbance. That's according to Joe.

DR. SEYMOUR: Joe?

DR. DOANE: Joe Palleni.

DR. SEYMOUR: A disturbance by singing? Singing "The Star-Spangled Banner"?

DR. DOANE: Yes. Joe handled it.

DR. SEYMOUR: Who is this Narwin woman?

DR. DOANE: An English teacher. She's been on the staff for years. Actually, longest of all, I think. A good teacher.

DR. SEYMOUR: Oh, yes. Think I know her. And that's all there is to it?

DR. DOANE: As far as I know.

DR. SEYMOUR: Let's hope so. I mean . . .

DR. DOANE: Al, no one could take this seriously.

DR. SEYMOUR: I hope not. I hope not. With the budget vote soon . . . and the school board—

**DR. DOANE:** Do you want me to call the newspaper?

**DR. SEYMOUR:** Ah . . . no. But if you get any calls you can refer them all to me. To my office. Tomorrow.

**DR. DOANE:** I will.

**DR. SEYMOUR:** This is not going to do us any good.

**DR. DOANE:** No one reads about schools.

**DR. SEYMOUR:** Let's hope so.

---

**9:20 A.M.**
**Phone Conversation**
**between Philip Malloy and Ken Barchet**

---

**PHILIP MALLOY:** What's happening?

**KEN BARCHET:** Did you see the paper?

**PHILIP MALLOY:** I deliver it. I don't have to read it.

**KEN BARCHET:** Guess what my ma found in it.

**PHILIP MALLOY:** What?

**KEN BARCHET:** It's all about you.

**PHILIP MALLOY:** Sure. April fool.

**KEN BARCHET:** No. Really. Look at section D. Page two. A riot.

**PHILIP MALLOY:** Sure.

**KEN BARCHET:** It ain't true. But it's funny. We working out?

**PHILIP MALLOY:** Have to visit my grandma at the nursing home.

**KEN BARCHET:** Make sure they don't lock you up. See you.

PHILIP MALLOY: Catch you later.

KEN BARCHET: Don't forget to look.

PHILIP MALLOY: April fool.

---

**9:50 A.M.**
**Conversation**
**between Philip Malloy's Parents**

---

MRS. MALLOY: Look here, Ben. That reporter did put in a story about Philip.

MR. MALLOY: You're kidding! Let me see.

MRS. MALLOY: Here.

MR. MALLOY: I'll be. . . .

MRS. MALLOY: It's got the whole thing.

MR. MALLOY: See, the superintendent says there's no such rule. It *was* just that teacher.

MRS. MALLOY: Doesn't seem right.

MR MALLOY: She should be fired. Philip upstairs?

MRS. MALLOY: Think so.

MR. MALLOY: Philip! Come on down here and look at this.

PHILIP MALLOY: What?

MRS. MALLOY: This.

MR. MALLOY: See. If you stick up for yourself, you get action. How's that make you feel? Philip? What do you think?

MRS. MALLOY: What's the matter?

PHILIP MALLOY: I don't know.

MRS. MALLOY: It was the teacher. Just as you said.

PHILIP MALLOY: Weird . . .

MR. MALLOY: Just shows you—

MRS. MALLOY: Where are you going?

PHILIP MALLOY: Upstairs.

MRS. MALLOY: We're leaving in half an hour.

MR. MALLOY: Sometimes you just have to deal with things.

MRS. MALLOY: He looked like he was reading his own funeral notice.

MR. MALLOY: Kids . . .

MRS. MALLOY: Well, anyway, you were right. Now maybe the boy can go back to school on Monday. Isn't it odd to see your name in the paper?

MR. MALLOY: I sort of like it. Good if Dexter sees it.

MRS. MALLOY: That Ted Griffen. He knows how to get things done.

MR. MALLOY: Got my vote.

---

**2:30 P.M.**
**Phone Conversation**
**between Margaret Narwin and Her Sister,**
**Anita Wigham**

---

MARGARET NARWIN: I just don't understand why they would ever print such a thing.

ANITA WIGHAM: That's the papers. . . .

MARGARET NARWIN: It's so slanted.

ANITA WIGHAM: Peg, I don't think anybody will pay much attention to it. Just tell people the truth. Put your faith in that.

MARGARET NARWIN: I suppose you're right. It's just . . .

ANITA WIGHAM: It will pass.

---

**7:30 P.M.**
**From a Speech Delivered by Ted Griffen
to a Meeting of the Harrison
Sunday Fellowship**

---

MR. GRIFFEN: . . . so what I will try to do—if elected as a member of the Harrison School Board—is not just keep the cost of education down to a reasonable level—keeping our taxes down—I will work with the rest of the board to support basic American values. For I—and I can only speak for myself—I am shocked that a Harrison student should be suspended from one of our schools because he desires to sing the national anthem. Yes, my friends, it is true. It has happened here. Here—in today's *Record*—is the sad story. And I say, what is the point of installing computers—which my generation never seemed to need—and at great cost—if our young people are not allowed to practice the elemental values of American patriotism?

## 11:20 P.M.
## From the Diary of Philip Malloy

Folks excited—mostly Dad—by a newspaper story about what happened in school. Wonder what will happen now. Dad keeps telling me how great I am.

Maybe they'll kick Miss Narwin out. Wonder if she even saw it. It's her fault. Not mine.

No one called. I guess I don't go to school tomorrow.

Watched some track on TV. Steve Hallick lost a race. Said he wasn't ready. Can't believe it.

Finished *The Outsiders*. Not bad. Wonder what it would be like to live without parents. You could do what you'd like.

# Chapter 15

Monday, April 2

## From American Affiliated Press Wire Service

## KICKED OUT OF SCHOOL FOR PATRIOTISM

*Harrison, NH.* A tenth grader was suspended from his local school because he sang "The Star-Spangled Banner" during the school's morning exercises. The boy, Philip Malloy, who wished to sing in the spirit of patriotism, was then forced to remain home alone, since both his parents work. English teacher Margaret Narwin, who brought about the suspension, maintains the boy was making a nuisance of himself.

## 8:05 A.M. Transcript from the Jake Barlow Talk Show

JAKE BARLOW: Okay. Okay. Here we go! All sorts of things we can talk about. Wanting—and waiting—to hear from you on WLRB, your talk radio with your loudmouthed host Jake Barlow ready to take you on. Ready. Willing. And able! All kinds of things going on. We can talk about that demonstration in Washington. I don't know about that. I don't know. Bunch of . . . Hey, what do you think about that point-shaving scandal over at that university in the Midwest? Come on, guys, is that an education or what? Then there's the president, who's said he would *be* an education president. But he's got his work cut out for him. I'm telling you because here's a bit of a story, bit of a story, that came in over the wires. Don't know if you saw this. Let me read it to you. Now, listen up! This is America. I mean it! WLRB asking you—Jake Barlow asking you—what you think of *this*. Now, remember, I'm not making this up. None of it. I'm *reading* it!

"KICKED OUT OF SCHOOL FOR PATRIOTISM."

Right. You heard me correct. "KICKED OUT OF SCHOOL FOR PATRIOTISM." But you ain't heard nothing yet. Listen to this!

"Harrison, New Hampshire."

Where in the *world* is Harrison? In the United States? In America? Listen up, New Hampshire. All their auto plates read "Live free or die." Well, something died, because this is what is going on there right now! Here it is. The whole story. Right in the morning news. I'm just quoting.

"A tenth grader was suspended from his local school because he sang 'The Star-Spangled Banner' during the school's morning exercises. The boy, Philip Malloy, who wished to sing in the spirit of patriotism, was then forced to remain home alone, since both his parents work. English teacher Margaret Narwin, who brought about the suspension, maintains the boy was making a nuisance of himself."

Would you believe it? Would you believe it. Okay, this is WLRB, all-talk radio. Take a short break, then come right back to talk about whatever you want. Man, but I'm telling you: what's happening to this country!

Now this. . . .

---

**8:07 A.M.**
**Phone Conversation between**
**Mrs. Gloria Harland, Chairman,**
**Harrison School Board,**
**and Dr. Albert Seymour,**
**Superintendent of Schools**

---

MRS. HARLAND: Albert, this is Gloria Harland. Good morning.

DR. SEYMOUR: Gloria! Good morning. Looks like spring is here.

MRS. HARLAND: It is balmy, isn't it? Albert, last night I attended a meeting of the Harrison Sunday Fellowship. . . .

DR. SEYMOUR: Oh, yes. Couldn't make it.

MRS. HARLAND: Well, Ted Griffen made a speech.

DR. SEYMOUR: Ted Griffen?

MRS. HARLAND: He's running for the school board.

DR. SEYMOUR: Oh, yes. Right. They're doing a series of talks. Know him. Know him well. Bit hard and—

MRS. HARLAND: Albert, part of Ted's speech was an attack on the present board in regard to what he claims is the suspension of a student for singing the national anthem in one of the schools. High school, I think.

DR. SEYMOUR: The what?

MRS. HARLAND: Suspension for singing the national anthem. "The Star-Spangled Banner." And—to my shock—I checked and sure enough, as he said, I saw something about it in the paper yesterday. The Sunday paper. What *is* this all about? We have the vote . . .

DR. SEYMOUR: Oh, Lord, is he going to make a thing about this?

MRS. HARLAND: What happened? It's not true, is it?

DR. SEYMOUR: Gloria, I can assure you nothing of the kind occurred. Nothing. But before I go off half-cocked, let me make some further inquiries and then get back to you.

MRS. HARLAND: Soon.

DR. SEYMOUR: Absolutely. Soon.

MRS. HARLAND: Al, this is *not* what we need. Not with the budget vote so—

DR. SEYMOUR: Exactly. I understand.

---

**8:10 A.M.**
**Transcript**
**from the Jake Barlow Talk Show**

---

JAKE BARLOW: Okay. Okay. Back again. And ready to take you on. We've got the scandal out at the U. The demonstration in D.C. The kid kicked out of school for being an American patriot. Anything you want. Here we go. First call. Hello?

**CALLER:** Is this Jake?

**JAKE BARLOW:** Jake Cruising-for-a-Bruising Barlow. Who's this?

**CALLER:** This is Steve.

**JAKE BARLOW:** Steve! How you doing, big guy?

**STEVE:** Great. Really like your show. You're doing great.

**JAKE BARLOW:** Don't tell me! Tell the president of the station, Steve.

**STEVE:** Yeah. Ha-ha! Right. Look—about that kid.

**JAKE BARLOW:** The one kicked out of school for singing "The Star-Spangled Banner"?

**STEVE:** Yeah. Hey, you know, that gripes me. Really does. Things may be different. But, come off it!

**JAKE BARLOW:** Right! What are schools for, anyway?

**STEVE:** People might call me a—a—

**JAKE BARLOW:** Jerk?

**STEVE:** Yeah, maybe. But like they used to say, America, love it or leave it. And that school—

**JAKE BARLOW:** It was a teacher.

**STEVE:** Yeah, teacher. She shouldn't be allowed to teach. That's my opinion.

**JAKE BARLOW:** Right. I'm right with you there, Steve. I mean, there are the three R's—reading, 'riting, and 'rithmetic—and the three P's—prayer, patriotism, and parents. At least, that's my notion of schooling.

**STEVE:** Right. I'm right with you.

JAKE BARLOW: Okay, Steve. Like what you said. Let's see if we got any ultraliberals out there who'll call in and try to defend this—I was about to say *woman*—person. Steve! Thanks for calling.

STEVE: Yeah.

JAKE BARLOW: Who's next?

---

**8:30 A.M.**
**Conversation**
**between Dr. Albert Seymour and**
**Dr. Gertrude Doane**

---

DR. SEYMOUR: Gert, Albert Seymour here. Look, I got a call from Gloria Harland about this boy who was suspended for singing.

DR. DOANE: Al, I told you, that's *not* why the boy was suspended.

DR. SEYMOUR: Maybe yes. Maybe no. That's not what's at stake here. I've got this budget. . . . Now listen. She was at a meeting last night at which this guy, Ted Griffen—

DR. DOANE: He's running for the school board.

DR. SEYMOUR: Exactly. And wouldn't you know, he's making speeches about the incident, claiming it's school policy to keep kids from singing—

DR. DOANE: Al, that's absolutely untrue.

DR. SEYMOUR: Gert, you know as well as I, it doesn't matter if it's true or not true. It's what people are saying that's important. Will be saying. Who's involved in this thing?

126    Literature Connections

DR. DOANE: Joe Palleni, Peg Narwin, myself.

DR. SEYMOUR: I want a report on my desk—a report I can read out. So make it short and to the point. Soon as you can.

DR. DOANE: Al . . .

DR. SEYMOUR: Gert, believe me. I'm sensitive to this sort of thing. Just do as I've requested.

---

**8:35 A.M.**
**Transcript**
**from the Jake Barlow Talk Show**

---

JAKE BARLOW: Okay. Who's this?

CALLER: My name is Liz.

JAKE BARLOW: Liz baby! How you doing?

LIZ: Just fine.

JAKE BARLOW: Liz, what's on your pretty mind this morning?

LIZ: Jake, I'm a mother. I have three kids. All school-age. But if I had a teacher like that—

JAKE BARLOW: Whoa! Back off. Like who?

LIZ: The one who forbade that child to show his patriotism in school. . . .

JAKE BARLOW: Right.

LIZ: I'd take my kids out of school.

JAKE BARLOW: You would?

LIZ: No question about it.

**JAKE BARLOW:** What about the teacher?

**LIZ:** Wouldn't let my kids go back to that school unless she was removed.

**JAKE BARLOW:** The teacher doesn't have rights?

**LIZ:** It's a free country. But what I'm saying is that she has no right to do what she does. My husband was in the military. She's taking away rights. Like the flag thing.

**JAKE BARLOW:** Then you know.

**LIZ:** I do.

---

**9:17 A.M.**
**Conversation between Robert Duval,**
**Reporter for the *St. Louis Post-Dispatch*,**
**and Dr. Gertrude Doane**

---

**MR. DUVAL:** Is this Miss Doane, principal of Harrison High School?

**DR. DOANE:** Yes. Dr. Doane.

**MR. DUVAL:** Thank you. Of course. Dr. Doane, my name is Robert Duval. I'm a reporter with the *St. Louis Post-Dispatch.*

**DR. DOANE:** St. Louis?

**MR. DUVAL:** That's right. I'm calling from St. Louis, Missouri. I'm attempting to follow up on an AAP release that indicates your school suspended a student because he sang "The Star-Spangled Banner."

**DR. DOANE:** Did you say St. Louis?

**MR. DUVAL:** Yes, ma'am. Took the story off the wire service. And we ran it. Now you see, we have a convention going on here, our state American Legion convention. Someone there noticed this item and called the paper to see if we had any more information about the situation.

**DR. DOANE:** Are you serious?

**MR. DUVAL:** Certainly am. Would you care to hear the story we ran?

**DR. DOANE:** Ah . . . yes.

**MR. DUVAL:** The headline reads "KICKED OUT OF SCHOOL FOR PATRIOTISM."

**DR. DOANE:** Good grief!

**MR. DUVAL:** Yes, ma'am. Let me read you the rest. "Harrison, New Hampshire. A tenth grader was suspended from his local school because he sang 'The Star-Spangled Banner' during the school's morning exercises. The boy, Philip Malloy, who wished to sing in the spirit of patriotism, was then forced to remain home alone, since both his parents work. English teacher Margaret Narwin, who brought about the suspension, maintains the boy was making a nuisance of himself." That's it.

**DR. DOANE:** My God. . . . Is that being sent out over the whole country?

**MR. DUVAL:** Well, actually, *has* been sent out. And I thought to call and get your response. Would you like to comment, ma'am?

**DR. DOANE:** Full of mistakes. For a start he's a *ninth* grader. . . . Look, can I get back to you?

**MR. DUVAL:** Aren't you in a position to respond now?

DR. DOANE: There has been some great mistake, and . . . None of this is true.

MR. DUVAL: None of it? The boy was not suspended, then?

DR. DOANE: Yes, suspended, but not for those reasons. Look, Mr. Duval, I have to sort this out.

MR. DUVAL: When can I call back?

DR. DOANE: Give me a few hours.

MR. DUVAL: Yes, ma'am.

---

**9:32 A.M.**
**Transcript**
**from the Jake Barlow Talk Show**

---

JAKE BARLOW: Back again. Who's on?

CALLER: This is Roger.

JAKE BARLOW: Roger Rabbit?

ROGER: Not quite.

JAKE BARLOW: How many kids do you have?

ROGER: Ahhh . . . two.

JAKE BARLOW: Get hopping, Roger, get hopping. Ha! Okay, Roger, what's on your mind?

ROGER: About all these calls you're getting, the boy who was kicked out.

JAKE BARLOW: Makes me sick. *Sick!*

ROGER: Well, you've read the news story a few times, so I think I've understood it. And it just seems to me that that couldn't be the whole story.

**JAKE BARLOW:** What do you mean?

**ROGER:** Well, the story is slanted from the point of view of the boy. It doesn't really indicate what the teacher's position is.

**JAKE BARLOW:** Roger—let me get this right—you are defending this so-called teacher?

**ROGER:** No, I didn't say that. I'm not defending anyone. The story you read is just the boy's, not the teacher's. Why should we assume that the teacher is wrong?

**JAKE BARLOW:** Come on. Give us a break. The kid was suspended, right?

**ROGER:** So it would appear.

**JAKE BARLOW:** Suspended for singing the national anthem, right?

**ROGER:** That's the story you read.

**JAKE BARLOW:** Now, how could singing the national anthem—*Oh, say, can you see . . .*—ever . . . ever . . . ever be making a nuisance?

**ROGER:** Well . . .

**JAKE BARLOW:** Roger, what's your point? Let me make a guess. You're a teacher!

**ROGER:** Actually, I'm a salesman.

**JAKE BARLOW:** What do you sell?

**ROGER:** That doesn't make—

**JAKE BARLOW:** Come on! Out with it! Admit it.

**ROGER:** Well, books, but . . .

**JAKE BARLOW:** Yeah, see, exactly. And here you are

defending this *creep* of a teacher. What does the kid know other than his own, natural-born patriotism? And then this creep of a teacher comes along and squelches it. And this country has all these problems with morality, drugs, pornography. No way, José. Hey, Roger, you saying pornography is only a nuisance?

ROGER: But—

JAKE BARLOW: Good-bye! Always the one rotten apple. Hey, out there. Do you agree with this guy? Tell you what! Why don't you out there—let's start a crusade—I want you all—if you feel anything about all this—to *write* to the teacher. Hey, free country! Do you agree with what she did? Okay, tell her. If you disagree, tell her that. Let's see, here's her name, Margaret Narwin. Margaret Narwin. N-a-r-w-i-n. Harrison, New Hampshire. Let her know what you think. You agree with that guy? Just write her. Postcard. *Brick*. Hey, just kidding. Something. Okay! Now this. . . .

---

**10:00 A.M.
Conversation
among Dr. Gertrude Doane,
Margaret Narwin,
and Dr. Joseph Palleni**

---

DR. DOANE: Peg, just tell me what happened.

MISS NARWIN: I've told you twice now.

DR. DOANE: I know you're upset, Peg. But I have to get it down clearly. Anyway, we all need to tell the same story.

**DR. PALLENI:** Amen. Gert's trying to be helpful, Peg.

**MISS NARWIN:** It's terribly upsetting.

**DR. DOANE:** Well, yes. . . . To all of us. Now, once more. Please.

**MISS NARWIN:** Very well. . . . Philip Malloy—from the first day he entered my homeroom—last week—during the time the students are asked to stand in silence—

**DR. PALLENI:** The rule is, "Respectful silence." I looked it up. It's in your memo about opening exercises. Isn't in the student handbook. But I think it should be.

**DR. DOANE:** Good point.

**MISS NARWIN:** During the playing of the national anthem, he sang loudly. With no respect. Very loudly. To make a commotion. Obviously. The first time he did it, I asked him to stop, and he did. After a bit. The second two times, he didn't. Refused. That's when I sent him to Joe. Both times.

**DR. PALLENI:** The boy admitted it, Gert. No bones about that.

**MISS NARWIN:** Deliberately provocative.

**DR. DOANE:** Do we know why? Peg?

**MISS NARWIN:** I haven't the slightest idea.

**DR. DOANE:** Joe?

**DR. PALLENI:** Nope. No problems before. Ever.

**DR. DOANE:** Maybe I should talk to some students.

**DR. PALLENI:** Witnesses.

**MISS NARWIN:** I don't know. I will say this, Gert, he's always been restless in English class. Sort of a wise guy, I'd have to call him. Trying to cover up laziness with smart talk. I don't know why. Sometimes that just happens. The chemistry. In his last exam for me he wrote a very foolish, really provocative, answer. Mocking me.

**DR. DOANE:** You?

**MISS NARWIN:** Oh, yes. Absolutely. Mocking.

**DR. DOANE:** Do you still have it?

**MISS NARWIN:** I always return exams to students.

**DR. DOANE:** Too bad. But there must be some reason—

**MISS NARWIN:** I agree.

**DR. PALLENI:** Home, Gert. Home. Ninety-nine point nine times out of a hundred, you get a thing like this, a kid acting out, believe me, it's home. Acting out here for what's happening there.

**DR. DOANE:** But we don't know that.

**DR. PALLENI:** Hey, what's the difference? They always blame the school. You know that.

**DR. DOANE:** Well, as far as I'm concerned, this is strictly a discipline problem. That's what I intend to tell people. Do we agree?

**DR. PALLENI:** Well, the thing is, it's the truth.

**MISS NARWIN:** I didn't think it was wise to suspend him.

**DR. PALLENI:** Two infractions in one week, Peg. Right? That's the rule. You sent him out. To me. If we start bending the rules each time . . .

**MISS NARWIN:** What could I have done?

DR. PALLENI: Only trying to be supportive.

MISS NARWIN: I know.

DR. DOANE: It'll blow over.

DR. PALLENI: Sure thing.

DR. DOANE: Joe, write up a draft of something—keep strictly to the facts—to give to Seymour. Do it immediately. I want to speak to some students.

---

**11:00 A.M.**
**Written by Dr. Joseph Palleni**

---

## MEMO

### HARRISON SCHOOL DISTRICT

Where Our Children Are Educated,
Not Just Taught

Dr. Albert Seymour  Mrs. Gloria Harland
*Superintendent* *Chairman, School Board*

TO: SEYMOUR
FROM: DOANE
RE: SUSPENSION OF PHILIP MALLOY

1. Each morning—during homeroom period—the national anthem is played over the high school announcement system.

2. At such times students are asked: "Please all rise and stand at *respectful, silent* attention . . ."

3. On March 28, March 29, and March 30, Philip Malloy caused a disturbance in his homeroom class (Margaret Narwin, teacher) by singing the national anthem in a loud, raucous, *disrespectful* manner.

4. When asked by Miss Narwin—on the first occasion—to cease, Philip Malloy reluctantly did so. But on the second and third occasions, he refused and was sent to Assistant Principal Joe Palleni for discipline.

5. Philip Malloy does not dispute the above facts.

6. On the third occurrence, Philip Malloy was asked to promise not to show such a disrespectful attitude, and to apologize to the teacher and to his fellow classmates. He refused.

7. Dr. Palleni, following his principal's guidelines, therefore suspended Philip Malloy from class for two days in hopes that he would learn to show proper respect toward the national anthem, school, teacher, and fellow students.

8. It should be noted that Philip Malloy was reported to show inappropriate behavior in his regular English classes with Miss Narwin.

DR. DOANE: Ken, I'm trying to understand what happened there. That morning. Is this clear?

KEN BARCHET: Yes.

DR. DOANE: And you were with him. I hope you can speak freely. I'm just trying to work it out.

KEN BARCHET: Sure.

DR. DOANE: So, in your view—what occurred?

KEN BARCHET: Well, you know, the tape, the music went on—

DR. DOANE: Which day was this?

KEN BARCHET: Wednesday.

DR. DOANE: Okay. Wednesday. Go on.

KEN BARCHET: Right. The music went on. And we were just standing there. We're supposed to. And the next thing, Miss Narwin was telling Philip to stop.

DR. DOANE: Stop what?

KEN BARCHET: I'm not sure. The newspaper said singing.

DR. DOANE: What about the other days?

KEN BARCHET: You know, he was, again, sort of, I guess, singing.

DR. DOANE: In what way?

KEN BARCHET: Just singing.

**DR. DOANE:** Loudly?

**KEN BARCHET:** Well, not really.

**DR. DOANE:** But you heard him?

**KEN BARCHET:** I guess.

**DR. DOANE:** How close to Philip do you sit?

**KEN BARCHET:** 'Cross the room.

**DR. DOANE:** So, loudly enough for you to hear?

**KEN BARCHET:** Well . . .

**DR. DOANE:** Then what happened?

**KEN BARCHET:** Miss Narwin got mad.

**DR. DOANE:** Why?

**KEN BARCHET:** Well, you know, like you said, Philip was singing. And I guess we're not supposed to.

**DR. DOANE:** Did Philip stop?

**KEN BARCHET:** Yeah. When she told him to get out.

**DR. DOANE:** Not before?

**KEN BARCHET:** No.

**DR. DOANE:** What did the class do?

**KEN BARCHET:** I wasn't paying attention.

KEN BARCHET: Hey, man, what's happening?

PHILIP MALLOY: Nothing. It's boring. What's happening there?

KEN BARCHET: Just spoke to Doane.

PHILIP MALLOY: The principal?

KEN BARCHET: Yeah.

PHILIP MALLOY: How come?

KEN BARCHET: She called me in to find out what happened.

PHILIP MALLOY: What you tell her?

KEN BARCHET: What happened. The whole thing. Lot of people talking about it. You know, with the newspaper and all.

PHILIP MALLOY: Yeah, but what did you tell her?

KEN BARCHET: I thought I should tell her how funny it was.

PHILIP MALLOY: Come on! What did you tell her?

KEN BARCHET: Nothing. I mean, it wasn't anything. I don't know why they're making a fuss about it.

PHILIP MALLOY: I still have English with her, but they switched me back to Lunser's homeroom.

KEN BARCHET: He's okay. Tells good jokes. Someone told me he has a collection of joke books. That's where he gets all those one-liners.

PHILIP MALLOY: That true?

KEN BARCHET: Nick told me. We going to work out this afternoon?

PHILIP MALLOY: Yeah.

KEN BARCHET: Catch you later.

---

**11:50 A.M.**
**Conversation**
**between Dr. Gertrude Doane**
**and Cynthia Gambia, Student**

---

DR. DOANE: Cynthia, what I'm trying to do is understand what happened in Miss Narwin's homeroom class. With Philip Malloy. When these incidents occurred. I hope you can tell me exactly what you saw. I'm trying to work it out.

CYNTHIA GAMBIA: Yes. I understand. I wasn't paying much attention.

DR. DOANE: That's all right. Go on. Tell me what happened as you saw it.

CYNTHIA GAMBIA: Well, during "The Star-Spangled Banner"—when the tape went on—Philip started to hum.

DR. DOANE: *Hum?*

CYNTHIA GAMBIA: I think so.

DR. DOANE: Not sing?

CYNTHIA GAMBIA: I'm not sure. It could have been. I wasn't paying attention. Not at first. Not the first time.

DR. DOANE: And then?

**CYNTHIA GAMBIA:** Miss Narwin asked him to leave.

**DR. DOANE:** Which days were these?

**CYNTHIA GAMBIA:** All three.

**DR. DOANE:** Was Philip causing a disturbance?

**CYNTHIA GAMBIA:** Well, I heard him. Sort of. I mean, it wasn't loud or anything. Not like the paper said. But he wouldn't stop. And she did ask him. I guess that was the disturbance.

**DR. DOANE:** So he wasn't loud.

**CYNTHIA GAMBIA:** Maybe the last time.

**DR. DOANE:** Very loud?

**CYNTHIA GAMBIA:** Well, loud.

**DR. DOANE:** What day was that?

**CYNTHIA GAMBIA:** Ah . . . Tuesday. Or Thursday. I'm not sure.

**DR. DOANE:** What did the other students do?

**CYNTHIA GAMBIA:** Nothing. I don't think they knew anything was going to happen. If they did, they would have watched.

**DR. DOANE:** Do you have any idea why he—Philip—did this?

**CYNTHIA GAMBIA:** No.

**DR. DOANE:** Did you want to add anything else?

**CYNTHIA GAMBIA:** No. I guess not. I mean, he *was* being sort of rude.

**DR. DOANE:** Philip?

**CYNTHIA GAMBIA:** Miss Narwin did ask him to stop. You're supposed to be quiet. Everybody says that's the rule. He certainly wasn't. She's a fair teacher. All the kids say so.

---

**12:30 P.M.**
**From a Speech Delivered by Ted Griffen to a Lunch Meeting of the Harrison Rotary Club**

---

MR. GRIFFEN: . . . so what I will try to do—if elected as a member of the Harrison School Board—is not just keep the cost of education down to a reasonable level—I'm talking here of keeping our taxes down—I will work with the rest of the board to support basic American values. But let me tell you good people—and I am sure I speak for you too—I am shocked that a Harrison student should be expelled from one of our schools simply because he desires to sing the national anthem. Yes, my friends, it is true. It has happened here. Here—in yesterday's *Record* is the full story. Shocking. What I say is—most emphatically—what is the point of installing computers—which my generation never seemed to need—and at great cost—if our young people are not allowed to practice the elemental values of American patriotism? Is that the way we budget our education dollars?

---

**12:50 P.M.**
**Conversation between Dr. Gertrude Doane and Allison Doresett**

---

DR. DOANE: Allison, I'm working hard to understand what happened in Miss Narwin's class. The incident with Philip Malloy.

**ALLISON DORESETT:** I know. Lot of kids are talking about it.

**DR. DOANE:** What are they saying?

**ALLISON DORESETT:** About how big a thing it is.

**DR. DOANE:** Do you think it is?

**ALLISON DORESETT:** I don't know. Maybe. If they pay all that attention. I mean, someone said the TV would be here.

**DR. DOANE:** I hope not. Now, as I understand it, you are in Miss Narwin's homeroom class.

**ALLISON DORESETT:** I have English with her too.

**DR. DOANE:** I'm talking about homeroom.

**ALLISON DORESETT:** I have her.

**DR. DOANE:** So you were there all three times?

**ALLISON DORESETT:** Uh-huh.

**DR. DOANE:** Tell me what you saw.

**ALLISON DORESETT:** Well, Philip, he doesn't like Miss Narwin.

**DR. DOANE:** He doesn't?

**ALLISON DORESETT:** I don't think so.

**DR. DOANE:** Just think? Do you know why?

**ALLISON DORESETT:** It's what people are saying. In class— English class—he just sits there, you know, like he's bored and can't stand anything she says. It's just the way he looks. On his face. You know. But then he suddenly makes some remark, a joke or something. Something funny.

**DR. DOANE:** Do you think this has anything to do with what happened?

**ALLISON DORESETT:** Well, it was so obvious he was trying to get at her.

**DR. DOANE:** What do you mean?

**ALLISON DORESETT:** Get her mad.

**DR. DOANE:** Because he doesn't like her?

**ALLISON DORESETT:** He's been so moody lately. Those times in homeroom—I think he was doing it to get Miss Narwin in trouble.

**DR. DOANE:** I wish you'd tell me more about that.

**ALLISON DORESETT:** Well, he's been angry a lot lately. I go home on the same bus with him. The other day I— you know—tried to sit next to him. On the bus. He was looking all angry. I tried to talk to him.

**DR. DOANE:** And?

**ALLISON DORESETT:** He got all angry. Wouldn't talk to me.

**DR. DOANE:** Do you know why?

**ALLISON DORESETT:** That's the way he is.

**DR. DOANE:** Allison, I appreciate your help.

**ALLISON DORESETT:** Can I say something?

**DR. DOANE:** Of course.

**ALLISON DORESETT:** I like Miss Narwin.

**DR. DOANE:** I'm glad. Your telling the truth can only help her.

## MEMO

### HARRISON SCHOOL DISTRICT

Where Our Children Are Educated,
Not Just Taught

Dr. Albert Seymour  Mrs. Gloria Harland
*Superintendent* *Chairman, School Board*

TO: DR. A. SEYMOUR
FROM: DR. G. DOANE
RE: SUSPENSION OF PHILIP MALLOY

1. Each and every morning—during homeroom period—the national anthem is played over the high school announcement system.

2. At such times all students are asked, to quote the standard district guide, "Please all rise and stand at *respectful,* silent attention. . . ." At no time in the history of this procedure has any disturbance been recorded.

3. On March 28, March 29, and March 30, Philip Malloy deliberately caused a disturbance in his homeroom class (Margaret Narwin, teacher) by singing the national anthem in a loud, raucous, *disrespectful* fashion, thereby drawing attention to himself.

4. When requested by Miss Narwin—on the first occasion—to cease, Philip Malloy did so, albeit reluctantly. On the second and third occasions, he repeated his disrespectful behavior, and when he refused to stop, he was sent—standard procedure—to Assistant Principal Dr. Joseph Palleni for discipline.

5. Philip Malloy did not dispute the above facts.

6. A random selection of students—who were in the classroom at the time—confirms these events. Indeed, there is evidence that Philip Malloy's acts were indicative of some personal animosity he feels toward the homeroom teacher, Miss Narwin. His rudeness was also on display in the English classes he had with her. His grade there indicates inferior work.

7. On the third occurrence, Philip Malloy was asked 1) to promise not to show such a disrespectful attitude toward our national anthem and 2) to apologize to his teacher and his classmates for his behavior. He refused, choosing the option afforded him of suspension.

8. Dr. Palleni, following district guidelines approved by the Superintendent, therefore suspended Philip Malloy from class for two days in hopes that he would learn to show proper respect toward the national anthem, his school, his teacher, and his fellow students.

Dr. Gertrude Doane
*Principal*

TO: MARGARET NARWIN, HARRISON,
NEW HAMPSHIRE, HIGH SCHOOL
FROM: YOUNG AMERICANS FOR AMERICA

On behalf of our membership we strongly condemn your suppression of patriotism in the American School System.

Sincerely,
Jessica Wittington, Executive Secretary
Tampa, Florida

TO: PHILIP MALLOY
FROM: SOCIETY FOR THE PRESERVATION
OF FREE SPEECH

We applaud your defense of the freedom of speech in a public arena. One is never too young to fight for our constitutional rights, which are under constant assault from right-wing forces. Stand firm. Stand tall. Please call upon us for active support.

Hank Morgan
Chicago, Illinois

TO: PRINCIPAL, HARRISON HIGH

People like Margaret Marwin should be kicked out of teaching.

Charles Elderson
Woodbank, North Carolina

## MEMO

---

### HARRISON SCHOOL DISTRICT

Where Our Children Are Educated,
Not Just Taught

Dr. Albert Seymour  Mrs. Gloria Harland
*Superintendent* *Chairman, School Board*

TO: MRS. GLORIA HARLAND,
      CHAIRMAN, SCHOOL BOARD
FROM: DR. A. SEYMOUR
RE: SUSPENSION OF PHILIP MALLOY

1.  It is the practice in *all* Harrison schools that each and every morning—during homeroom

period—the national anthem is played over the announcement systems. It is part of our general ongoing program of support for traditional American values.

2. At such times all students are asked to "Please all rise and stand at *respectful,* silent attention. . . ." In past years our desire for a dignified moment of patriotism has been firmly maintained. At no time in the history of this program has any disturbance been recorded.

3. On March 28, March 29, and March 30, Philip Malloy deliberately caused a disturbance in his homeroom class (Margaret Narwin, a teacher of twenty years' standing) by singing the national anthem in a loud, raucous, *disrespectful* fashion, thereby drawing attention to himself and away from the words. There are strong indications that he was acting out some personal animosity toward the teacher in question for reasons unknown. His school performance has been inferior. (It has been suggested that there may be problems in the home arena. Please note, however, that the law *requires* schools to keep such personal information confidential.)

4. When requested by his teacher, Miss Narwin, on the first occasion to maintain a dignified response to the national anthem, Philip Malloy did so, though reluctantly. On the second and third occasions, he repeated his disrespectful acts, and when he refused to stop, he was—as a matter of course—sent to

Assistant Principal Dr. Joseph Palleni for discipline.

5. Philip Malloy—when given the opportunity—did *not* dispute the above facts.

6. Students who were in the classroom at the time of the incidents confirm these events.

7. On the third occurrence, Philip Malloy was requested 1) to promise that he would show an attitude of respect toward our national anthem and 2) to apologize to his teacher and his classmates for his rude behavior. He refused, choosing the option of suspension *himself.*

8. Dr. Palleni, following district guidelines approved by the School Board, therefore suspended Philip Malloy from class for two days in hopes that he would learn to show proper respect toward the national anthem and his school, teacher, and fellow students.

Dr. A. Seymour
*Superintendent of Schools*

---

**6:20 P.M.**
**Conversation**
**between Philip Malloy's Parents**

MR. MALLOY: Hi! Where's Philip?

MRS. MALLOY: He just got in. Washing up.

MR. MALLOY: People were talking about him today. Amazing how many folks saw that thing in the paper.

MRS. MALLOY: At my place too.

MR. MALLOY: Makes you feel good.

MRS. MALLOY: We should celebrate.

---

**6:35 P.M.**
**Discussion**
**between Philip Malloy and His Parents**
**During Dinner**

---

MR. MALLOY: Well, how do you feel?

PHILIP MALLOY: Okay.

MRS. MALLOY: You should be pleased with yourself.

MR. MALLOY: What do you think of that telegram?

PHILIP MALLOY: I don't know. Who are they? I never heard of them before.

MR. MALLOY: They've heard of you. You're famous.

PHILIP MALLOY: How?

MRS. MALLOY: In the news, wasn't it?

PHILIP MALLOY: You think so?

MR. MALLOY: Sure. Just shows you. One person makes a difference. One person standing up for what he believes in.

MRS. MALLOY: I'm just so glad it's worked out all right. Aren't you?

PHILIP MALLOY: I suppose.

**MR. MALLOY:** What's the problem now?

**PHILIP MALLOY:** Be weird going back. What kids will say.

**MR. MALLOY:** They'll be on your side. You said they all hated that woman. Just make sure you sing in the morning. People will look to that.

**PHILIP MALLOY:** I'll be in Mr. Lunser's class.

**MR. MALLOY:** You said he likes kids singing.

**PHILIP MALLOY:** Sort of.

**MR. MALLOY:** I think you should go over and speak to Ted Griffen too.

**PHILIP MALLOY:** Why?

**MR. MALLOY:** Someone at work heard him at some speech he gave—the school board thing—he mentioned this whole business. . . .

**PHILIP MALLOY:** He did?

**MRS. MALLOY:** And he brought in that reporter.

**MR. MALLOY:** Come on, Philip, people are really on your side!

**PHILIP MALLOY:** I guess.

---

**7:30 P.M.**
**From a Speech Delivered by Ted Griffen**
**to a Meeting of the Harrison**
**Chamber of Commerce**

---

**MR. GRIFFEN:** Before I get into my formal speech, I'd like to lead off—put it right at the top of your thoughts—with something that has happened here in Harrison, something that has disturbed me greatly. I am a great believer in basic American values. And let me tell you good people—and I am sure I speak for you too—I am shocked that a Harrison student should be expelled from one of our schools because he desires to sing the national anthem. Yes, my friends, it is the truth. It has happened here. Here—in yesterday's *Record* is the full story. Shocking. What I say is—most emphatically—what is the point of installing computers—which my generation never seemed to need—and at great cost—if our young people are not allowed to practice the elemental values of American patriotism? And to think—because this story—so I understand—this has been picked up by the national press—how shocking it is that this is the way our town of Harrison should come to be known. It should not be condoned!

---

**8:02 P.M.**
**Phone Conversation**
**between Margaret Narwin and Her Sister,**
**Anita Wigham**

---

MISS NARWIN: Hello?

ANITA WIGHAM: Peg!

MISS NARWIN: Anita, yes, dear, what is it? What's the matter?

ANITA WIGHAM: I . . . I . . .

MISS NARWIN: What is it?

ANITA WIGHAM: I was just reading the evening paper—and right on page one . . . is this story—it's this story about you!

MISS NARWIN: What are you talking about?

ANITA WIGHAM: It's right *here*.

MISS NARWIN: Are you sure?

ANITA WIGHAM: Absolutely sure. It must be everywhere.

MISS NARWIN: What does it say?

ANITA WIGHAM: I'll read it. It's so awful, Peg. It says, "KICKED OUT OF SCHOOL FOR PATRIOTISM." That's the headline. It's just one of those boxed stories. But it's on the front page. "Harrison, New Hampshire. AAP. A tenth grader was suspended from his local school because he sang 'The Star-Spangled Banner' during the school's morning exercises. The boy, Philip Malloy, who wished to sing in the spirit of patriotism, was then forced to remain home alone, since both his parents work. English teacher Margaret Narwin, who brought about the suspension, maintains the boy was making a nuisance of himself." Peg, I don't understand. Peg?

MISS NARWIN: I . . .

ANITA WIGHAM: But why—

MISS NARWIN: And this was in your newspaper?

ANITA WIGHAM: Peg, I'm *holding* it.

MISS NARWIN: Dear God. . . .

ANITA WIGHAM: It's not true, is it?

MISS NARWIN: No. None of it.

ANITA WIGHAM: But where does it come from?

MISS NARWIN: Let me call you back. In a few moments.

DR. DOANE: Yes, Peg, hello. How are you?

MISS NARWIN: Gert, I . . .

DR. DOANE: Peg, are you all right?

MISS NARWIN: Gert, I just got a call from my sister—in Florida—about a newspaper story—published there—about this business—

DR. DOANE: I know, Peg. I've already heard about it.

MISS NARWIN: But I—

DR. DOANE: I just didn't see any point in upsetting you any more.

MISS NARWIN: But why?

DR. DOANE: I already received a call from some midwestern reporter. There have been telegrams—

MISS NARWIN: Telegrams?

DR. DOANE: At school. I told the office to hold them. Peg, it's gotten out of hand. I don't know how. It seems there are these radio talk shows—

MISS NARWIN: I want to see them. What do the telegrams say?

DR. DOANE: Well, they believe what the story says and . . . Believe me, Peg, I know. It's all a mistake.

MISS NARWIN: Were they addressed to me? Personally?

DR. DOANE: Well, to me, and yes, some to you, but—

MISS NARWIN: I want to see them.

DR. DOANE: I don't think—

MISS NARWIN: I don't understand any of this.

DR. DOANE: Peg, I assure you, I have complete confidence in you.

MISS NARWIN: It's so monstrous, so . . .

DR. DOANE: Yes, I agree.

MISS NARWIN: My sister, in Florida . . .

DR. DOANE: Peg, we're just going to have to weather it out and—maybe you'll want to take the day off tomorrow.

MISS NARWIN: No. I can't give in to this—

DR. DOANE: Peg, believe me. It will calm down.

---

### 10:33 P.M.
### From the Diary of Philip Malloy

---

Weird day not doing much. Got these telegrams from these people I never heard of before, talking about something I don't get. Folks all high. Be glad to be back in school. I hate sitting around. Glad to be in Lunser's homeroom class again. Get things back to normal. Guess I'll still be in Narwin's English. Better speak to her and see if I can do some extra work. So I can get on the track team. Wonder what she'll say?

Did some extra time on Dad's rowing machine.

I'm a little nervous.

# Chapter 16

Tuesday, April 3

---

**Letter Sent to Margaret Narwin**

---

To Margaret Narwin,

These days there is so much talk about young people and education. It seems to me that people like you—who don't believe in patriotism—cause the problems. You should find a better profession for your lack of ability.

LINDA DORCHESTER
Ann Arbor, Michigan

---

**Letter Sent to Margaret Narwin**

---

Dear Margaret Narwin,

As a teacher in the Dayton, Ohio, school system for ten years, I am dismayed and horrified that in this day and age a colleague of mine should suspend a student from school for singing the national anthem. We suffer enough from unfair criticism. The profession does not need people like you who make it so hard for the rest of us.

CARLTON HAVEN
Dayton, Ohio

---

## Letter Sent to Margaret Narwin

---

Margaret Narwin,

I'm a veteran who fought for his country and gave his blood and I really hate people like you.

DAVID MAIK
Eugene, Oregon

---

## Letter Sent to Margaret Narwin

---

Margaret Narwin,

Surely you have something better to do with your classroom authority than attacking kids who express their love of our country.

LAURA JACOBS
San Diego, California

---

## 7:15 A.M.
## Conversation
## between Dr. Albert Seymour
## and Dr. Gertrude Doane
## in the Superintendent's Office

---

**DR. DOANE:** How many are there?

**DR. SEYMOUR:** Telegrams? Ten. Fifteen. I haven't counted exactly. I suspect more will be coming.

**DR. DOANE:** This one is from Idaho. Incredible!

**DR. SEYMOUR:** Every one of them demanding we fire this Narwin woman.

**DR. DOANE:** Not this one.

**DR. SEYMOUR:** Well, the overwhelming majority. And I had twelve calls at my home last night.

**DR. DOANE:** From whom?

**DR. SEYMOUR:** People in town, Gert. People who vote. They're outraged.

**DR. DOANE:** And they believe that story. . . .

**DR. SEYMOUR:** I'm beginning to believe it.

**DR. DOANE:** Al!

**DR. SEYMOUR:** What do you expect me to do?

**DR. DOANE:** Support Peg Narwin.

**DR. SEYMOUR:** A TV network wants to interview people.

**DR. DOANE:** You're not going to let them. . . .

**DR. SEYMOUR:** No. No. Protect the privacy of minors and all that stuff. From what I gather, talk-show hosts—radio—have picked the story up. . . . The board wants me to issue a statement. Gert, I have an appointment with this Ted Griffen at nine-fifteen.

**DR. DOANE:** Griffen is running for board. . . .

**DR. SEYMOUR:** Exactly. He's already made speeches about this business. Look, Gert, I'm sorry, but between you and me—quote me and I'll deny it—I don't care about the board. I can handle them. But the budget—I don't need to tell you. If we lose again . . .

**DR. DOANE:** I know.

**DR. SEYMOUR:** People scream if the kids are not educated. Then they scream if you ask for the money to do it.

**DR. DOANE:** I know.

**DR. SEYMOUR:** I want to see the file on this Narwin woman.

**DR. DOANE:** Why?

**DR. SEYMOUR:** I have to decide what to do.

**DR. DOANE:** Before your meeting with this Griffen?

**DR. SEYMOUR:** Exactly. When you get to your office, send one of the secretaries over here with it.

**DR. DOANE:** Al . . .

**DR. SEYMOUR:** Gert, my job is to make sure these kids get educated. Whatever it takes. Send it.

---

**7:30 A.M.**
**Conversation**
**between Philip Malloy and His Parents**
**During Breakfast**

---

**MR. MALLOY:** You don't have to be nervous about anything. You were right. The fact that they moved you out of that woman's class proves you were right.

**PHILIP MALLOY:** Just homeroom. I have English with her.

MRS. MALLOY: I'm sure she won't give you any more trouble.

PHILIP MALLOY: It's just the other kids. . . .

MR. MALLOY: You said they hated her too.

PHILIP MALLOY: Yeah. . . .

MRS. MALLOY: Do you want me to drive you?

PHILIP MALLOY: No. I'm meeting Ken.

MRS. MALLOY: You'll be fine.

MR. MALLOY: You know how to make it work?

PHILIP MALLOY: No.

MR. MALLOY: Same as I've told you. Half your runs are won at the start. Head up. Leap out of the blocks. Show them what you can do.

PHILIP MALLOY: Easy for you

MR. MALLOY: The only reason I didn't make it to the Olympics . . .

PHILIP MALLOY: I know.

MR. MALLOY: Biggest regret I've ever had was dropping out of college.

PHILIP MALLOY: You had to.

MR. MALLOY: I suppose.

MRS. MALLOY: Phil, you better go if you don't want to miss your bus.

7:40 A.M.
**Conversation
between Philip Malloy and Ken Barchet
on the Way to the School Bus**

**PHILIP MALLOY:** What's happening?

**KEN BARCHET:** Nothing. What's with you?

**PHILIP MALLOY:** Not much. We going to run this afternoon?

**KEN BARCHET:** Can't.

**PHILIP MALLOY:** How come?

**KEN BARCHET:** Got track team right after school. Coach told us it's going to be at least three hours. You really should have tried out, man. You know that Polanski kid?

**PHILIP MALLOY:** Brian Polanski?

**KEN BARCHET:** Right. Coach has him down for the 400.

**PHILIP MALLOY:** Can't do anything.

**KEN BARCHET:** Best we got. You could.

**PHILIP MALLOY:** Sure.

**KEN BARCHET:** You mad at the coach or something?

**PHILIP MALLOY:** No. Why?

**KEN BARCHET:** You should change your mind.

**PHILIP MALLOY:** About what?

**KEN BARCHET:** Being on the team.

PHILIP MALLOY: Yeah, I might. I got Mr. Lunser for homeroom.

KEN BARCHET: You told me.

PHILIP MALLOY: Want to know why I didn't go out for the team?

KEN BARCHET: Okay.

PHILIP MALLOY: Narwin.

KEN BARCHET: What she have to do with it?

PHILIP MALLOY: She almost flunked me in English. That meant I wasn't allowed to try out.

KEN BARCHET: That why you're mad at her?

PHILIP MALLOY: But I'm going to ask her if I can do extra work. For credit.

KEN BARCHET: Think she'll give it to you?

PHILIP MALLOY: I don't know. No reason she shouldn't. I'll ask.

KEN BARCHET: She might be mad at you.

PHILIP MALLOY: If you just tell them you're sorry, that's all . . . .

KEN BARCHET: Be great if you could get on the team.

PHILIP MALLOY: That's what I've been saying.

---

**7:45 A.M.**
**Conversation**
**between Margaret Narwin and**
**Dr. Gertrude Doane**

---

MISS NARWIN: I don't believe it.

**DR. DOANE:** It is incredible.

**MISS NARWIN:** How many telegrams are there?

**DR. DOANE:** Here?

**MISS NARWIN:** Yes.

**DR. DOANE:** Almost two hundred.

**MISS NARWIN:** There will be letters. . . .

**DR. DOANE:** Well . . . The superintendent's office put out a statement explaining the true situation.

**MISS NARWIN:** What did he say?

**DR. DOANE:** Peg, you have to accept the idea that it's all a misunderstanding.

**MISS NARWIN:** Easy for you to say.

**DR. DOANE:** You can't blame yourself. . . .

**MISS NARWIN:** I pleaded with Joe not to suspend him.

**DR. DOANE:** I know you said that. We've issued a statement. I think it's good.

**MISS NARWIN:** May I see it?

**DR. DOANE:** Of course. Here. What's the matter?

**MISS NARWIN:** This statement doesn't support me.

**DR. DOANE:** Peg, it does.

**MISS NARWIN:** Where?

**DR. DOANE:** Peg, understand that—

**MISS NARWIN:** Will the boy be in school today?

**DR. DOANE:** I suppose. . . . I need to tell you I said no to some TV people.

**MISS NARWIN:** No. Absolutely not.

**DR. DOANE:** Exactly. They can't come in without permission. Peg, do you want to take the day off?

**MISS NARWIN:** No. They'll come to my home.

**DR. DOANE:** It's perfectly understandable.

**MISS NARWIN:** Gert, I don't understand. I don't. I have been teaching—

**DR. DOANE:** People believe what they read.

**MISS NARWIN:** I have my class. . . .

**DR. DOANE:** Peg, as of this morning I've moved Philip from your English class. He's with Mr. Keegan.

**MISS NARWIN:** Why did you do that?

**DR. DOANE:** Probably for the best. . . .

**MISS NARWIN:** Best for whom?

**DR. DOANE:** For you. The boy—

**MISS NARWIN:** Gert, people will misconstrue.

**DR. DOANE:** We are trying to be evenhanded. . . .

**MISS NARWIN:** He's a student. I'm a teacher. Hands are not meant to be even.

**DR. DOANE:** That's my decision.

---

### 7:55 A.M.
### Conversation
### between Philip Malloy and Allison Doresett

---

**ALLISON DORESETT:** Philip!

**PHILIP MALLOY:** Oh, hi.

**ALLISON DORESETT:** I just want you to know that I think what you did was really mean.

**PHILIP MALLOY:** What?

**ALLISON DORESETT:** Narwin is one of the best teachers. All the kids say so. It's really embarrassing.

**PHILIP MALLOY:** What are you talking about?

**ALLISON DORESETT:** You were just doing that to annoy her.

**PHILIP MALLOY:** Who?

**ALLISON DORESETT:** Miss Narwin. Everybody knows it. She's so fair.

**PHILIP MALLOY:** That's not true! Well, if you're not even going to listen . . . !

---

### 8:00 A.M.

---

### MEMO

---

### HARRISON SCHOOL DISTRICT

Where Our Children Are Educated,
Not Just Taught

Dr. Albert Seymour  Mrs. Gloria Harland
*Superintendent*          *Chairman, School Boar*

### OFFICIAL STATEMENT

It is the practice in *all* Harrison schools that during morning exercises the national anthem is played, part of our program in support of

> traditional American values.
>
> There is *no* rule that prohibits a student from singing along if he/she so desires.
>
> The Harrison School District is pleased to *encourage* appropriate displays of patriotism.
>
> It is the responsibility of our classroom teachers to monitor student behavior in this regard.

---

**8:03 A.M.**
**Discussion**
**in Bernard Lunser's Homeroom Class**

---

**MR. LUNSER:** Let's go! Let's go! Seats! My God, it's Philip Malloy, Harrison High's own Uncle Sam. Take any empty seat, Philip. I'll set it later.

**INTERCOM VOICE OF DR. GERTRUDE DOANE, HARRISON HIGH PRINCIPAL:** Good morning to all students, faculty, and staff. Today is Tuesday, April 3. Today will be a Schedule B day.

**MR. LUNSER:** That's B for bozos, boys and girls. B!

**DR. DOANE:** Today in history: on this day, in the year 1366, King Henry IV of England was born.

**MR. LUNSER:** Not to be confused with a fifth of scotch.

**DR. DOANE:** Today in 1860, the pony express began.

**MR. LUNSER:** Faster than today's PO.

**DR. DOANE:** April 3, in 1961, actor Eddie Murphy was born.

**MR. LUNSER:** Eddie Murphy. My only competition.

**DR. DOANE:** Please all rise and stand at respectful, silent attention for the playing of our national anthem.

**MR. LUNSER:** Philip!

**PHILIP MALLOY:** What?

**MR. LUNSER:** You want to sing?

**STUDENT:** Yeah, sing!

**MR. LUNSER:** Keep the lip buttoned, Brian! Philip?

**PHILIP MALLOY:** No. . . .

**MR. LUNSER:** Okay. Just want to make sure your rights are protected.

*Oh, say, can you see by the dawn's early light,*

*What so proudly we hailed at the twilight's last gleaming?*

*Whose broad stripes and bright stars, thro' the perilous fight,*

*O'er the ramparts we watched were so gallantly streaming? . . .*

**MR. LUNSER:** You sure, Philip?

**PHILIP MALLOY:** Yeah. . . .

*And the rockets' red glare, the bombs bursting in air,*

*Gave proof thro' the night that our flag was still there.*

*Oh, say does that star-spangled banner yet wave*

*O'er the land of the free and the home of the brave?*

MR. DUVAL. But that's just it. I've heard your superintendent's statement.

DR. DOANE: Mr. Duval, I am trying to run a school here with more than four hundred students.

MR. DUVAL: Well, ma'am, I spoke to your local reporter, the woman who broke the story, Ms. Stewart? She gave it to me. Would you like me to quote from the statement?

DR. DOANE: Mr. Duval, I know what it says.

MR. DUVAL. Now, it's not exactly in support of your Miss Narwin, is it. Would you agree?

DR. DOANE: Mr. Duval, I really don't think there's anything more to say.

MR. DUVAL: What I'm hearing, ma'am, is that you're not altogether happy with the statement.

DR. DOANE: I did *not* say that.

MR. DUVAL: I understand. But wouldn't this teacher— this Miss Narwin—like her side of the story set out?

DR. DOANE: I can't speak for her. She's a fine person who—

MR. DUVAL: Dr. Doane, I hope I can understand your conflict. But if I'm understanding this correctly there's something like a shift going on here. Against the teacher. Now, I don't have to go through you. I could approach her.

DR. DOANE: Why are you so interested?

MR. DUVAL: I sense there's something more here. I'm not even sure what. I confess that interests me. I sure would appreciate your cooperation.

DR. DOANE: I would have to ask her.

MR. DUVAL: I understand. But I am prepared to fly East right away.

DR. DOANE: Give me your number again.

MR. DUVAL: Sure thing.

---

**8:16 A.M.**
**Conversations**
**between Philip Malloy and Students**
**in the Hallway on the Way to First Class**

---

TODD BECKER: Hey, Philip, what's happening, man?

PHILIP MALLOY: Nothing.

TODD BECKER: You going to have a press conference?

PHILIP MALLOY: Get off!

JOSEPH CRIPPENS: Look out! Here comes Uncle Sam! That's what Mr. Lunser called him.

AMY DEVER: What's it like to be famous?

SUSAN FOWLER: Newspapers and all . . .

PHILIP MALLOY: Come on. I have to get to class.

JOSEPH CRIPPENS: Let the big man go.

**JASON MARKS:** Hey, Philip? How come you went after Narwin? Todd Becker said it's because you were failing English! That true?

**PHILIP MALLOY:** I have a class!

**JOSEPH CRIPPENS:** Let Uncle Sam go.

---

### Letter Sent to Philip Malloy

---

Dear Philip,

We support your defense of America. Keep on singing. We all join in.

> ROLANDO MERCHAUL
> Red Oak, Iowa

---

### Lotter Sent to Philip Malloy

---

Dear Philip,

We, Miss Harbor's 4th grade class at the Robert Fulton School, like to sing "The Star-Spangled Banner" too. You can come to our school.

> MS. HARBOR'S 4TH GRADE CLASS
> Robert Fulton School
> Brooklyn, New York

TO: PHILIP MALLOY

American Legion Post #16 of Newport, Rhode Island, salutes you for your defense of American values. Fight the good fight. Thumbs-up!

---

**9:20 A.M.**
**Conversation**
**between Dr. Albert Seymour**
**and Ted Griffen,**
**Candidate, Harrison School Board**

---

DR. SEYMOUR: Mr. Griffen. Nice to meet you. Come right in.

MR. GRIFFEN: Thank you. Thank you very much.

DR. SEYMOUR: Get you some coffee?

MR. GRIFFEN: No, thanks.

DR. SEYMOUR: Looks like we're finally getting some decent weather.

MR. GRIFFEN: Absolutely.

DR. SEYMOUR: Look, Mr. Griffen—

MR. GRIFFEN: Call me Ted.

DR. SEYMOUR: Fine. Ted. I'm Al. Now, aside from wanting to get to meet you, Ted . . . I've heard you speak— couple of times—was very interested in what you had to say—I thought it would be a good idea— generally—to meet you, and sort of, talk things over.

**MR. GRIFFEN:** Al, I appreciate that.

**DR. SEYMOUR:** Now—what we've got here—well, the media—they never pay attention to us unless something bad—

**MR. GRIFFEN:** Right. I never trust anything that's in print.

**DR. SEYMOUR:** Exactly. The bottom line. But we've got these elections coming up—budget.

**MR. GRIFFEN:** And the board.

**DR. SEYMOUR:** Exactly. I have a policy—I strongly believe in this—that I'm prepared to work with anyone who's on that board—the people's voice, that sort of thing. And we all want that same thing.

**MR. GRIFFEN:** Educating the kids.

**DR. SEYMOUR:** Exactly. We share that. But the budget thing—

**MR. GRIFFEN:** Have to keep costs down.

**DR. SEYMOUR:** Absolutely. But, Ted, I'll be frank with you. All this publicity—negative publicity—isn't— won't—do us any good.

**MR. GRIFFEN:** I understand.

**DR. SEYMOUR:** And, you understand, that first budget was tight—and this second one—to the bone. Get any closer and we're scooping marrow. And I understand—no one wants to pay a cent more. But without that budget, education is in big trouble here in Harrison.

**MR. GRIFFEN:** People want to hold the line on taxes.

**DR. SEYMOUR:** I sympathize. I pay taxes too. But—again to be frank—there's been a real misunderstanding regarding this national anthem thing. It doesn't help.

MR. GRIFFEN: Very disturbing.

DR. SEYMOUR: Exactly. It is. Let me share some of the facts with you.

MR. GRIFFEN: That's all I'm looking for.

DR. SEYMOUR: I appreciate that. What the media has done is confuse certain things—

MR. GRIFFEN: Something is confused.

DR. SEYMOUR: Exactly. First, though, let me tell you so you're quite clear, we have *no* rule against singing the national anthem. Never have had. Never will. Not as long as I'm superintendent.

MR. GRIFFEN: But the boy was suspended.

DR. SEYMOUR: Just getting to that. What I suspect here— we've got—a personal problem.

MR. GRIFFEN: The boy? He seems—

DR. SEYMOUR: Now, Ted, I'm speaking in confidence.

MR. GRIFFEN: Sure.

DR. SEYMOUR: Then we understand. Ted, it's not the boy. It's the teacher.

MR. GRIFFEN: This Narwin gal?

DR. SEYMOUR: Exactly.

MR. GRIFFEN: Well, I thought . . . What kind—between you and me—what kind of problem?

DR. SEYMOUR: Okay. Let me quote from a letter she wrote—this was to her principal—just a few weeks ago—I can't give you a copy, you understand— privacy and all—

**MR. GRIFFEN:** I understand.

**DR. SEYMOUR:** But I can read a part of it to you—so you can understand what I'm up against.

**MR. GRIFFEN:** Sure. Go on.

**DR. SEYMOUR:** She says—this Narwin woman—yes, here—now, I'm quoting her. "The truth is . . . I feel that sometimes"—get this—"I am a little out of touch with contemporary teaching, and, just as important, the students who come before me." In other words, she's been around, what can I say, since history began.

**MR. GRIFFEN:** Oh boy. . . . You've got a problem there. Tenure.

**DR. SEYMOUR:** Exactly. The question is, what are you and I going to do about it?

---

### 12:30 P.M.
### Lunchroom Conversation
### between Philip Malloy and Todd Becker

---

**TODD BECKER:** You don't have to sit alone, you know.

**PHILIP MALLOY:** I'm okay.

**TODD BECKER:** Can I sit?

**PHILIP MALLOY:** Suit yourself.

**TODD BECKER:** What's happening?

**PHILIP MALLOY:** Nothing.

**TODD BECKER:** That true you're going to be on TV?

**PHILIP MALLOY:** Who told you that?

**TODD BECKER:** Susan Vogle.

**PHILIP MALLOY:** No way.

**TODD BECKER:** But you're famous, right? All that newspaper stuff.

**PHILIP MALLOY:** What you come over here for? Just to tease me?

**TODD BECKER:** Just trying to be friendly.

**PHILIP MALLOY:** Yeah. Sure. Stuff it.

**TODD BECKER:** Suit yourself.

---

**12:35 P.M.**
**Faculty Lunchroom**
**Conversation**
**between Margaret Narwin and Mr. Benison**

---

**MR. BENISON:** You okay, Peg?

**MISS NARWIN:** Bit of a headache.

**MR. BENISON:** I saw those telegrams.

**MISS NARWIN:** It's awful.

**MR. BENISON:** Yeah, well, it's a crazy world. Who's that guy who said everybody will be famous for a few minutes?

**MISS NARWIN:** Andy Warhol. I really can't stand this.

**MR. BENISON:** I know. Lot of people upset. That's for sure.

**MISS NARWIN:** What do you mean?

**MR. BENISON:** I must have had ten calls last night saying—neighbors, a couple of family people—

asking, is it true? I told them look, it wasn't anything like that. That you didn't mean it to happen that way.

MISS NARWIN: What did you say I meant?

MR. BENISON: You know, some personal thing, happens all the time. . . .

MISS NARWIN: That's not what it was! The boy was being rude!

MR. BENISON: Okay, Peg, I know that, but no one expected, you know, all this. . . . What people are saying, we'll never get our budget.

MISS NARWIN: I really don't want to talk about it anymore.

MR. BENISON: Now wait a minute. Peg . . . don't go off. . . .

---

**1:30 P.M.**
**Conversation**
**between Philip Malloy**
**and Margaret Narwin**

---

PHILIP MALLOY: Miss Narwin?

MISS NARWIN: Philip? What are you doing here? What do you want?

PHILIP MALLOY: My class.

MISS NARWIN: You're . . . you're not in this section anymore. You were switched.

PHILIP MALLOY: I was?

MISS NARWIN: You're in Mr. Keegan's class.

PHILIP MALLOY: But—

MISS NARWIN: What?

PHILIP MALLOY: To get my grade up—I was going to ask for extra work. . . .

MISS NARWIN: Philip, you are no longer in my class. Didn't you hear me?

PHILIP MALLOY: So I could get on the track team and . . .

MISS NARWIN: You are not in my class.

PHILIP MALLOY: But what about the grade?

MISS NARWIN: Please leave the room. I want you out. Sara, take this note to Dr. Doane. . . .

PHILIP MALLOY: But . . .

MISS NARWIN: You must leave. Go!

PHILIP MALLOY: I'm leaving.

MISS NARWIN: Speak to Dr. Doane. Now, please, leave!

---

**2:50 P.M.**
**Conversation**
**between Philip Malloy and Coach Jamison**

---

COACH JAMISON: Oh, Philip. Didn't see you there.

PHILIP MALLOY: Can I talk to you a minute?

COACH JAMISON: Yeah. Sure. Got a minute.

PHILIP MALLOY: Remember, you said I should ask Miss Narwin for some extra work. . . .

COACH JAMISON: Sure.

PHILIP MALLOY: So I could get my grade up, get on the team.

COACH JAMISON: Okay.

PHILIP MALLOY: She won't let me.

COACH JAMISON: She won't let you what?

PHILIP MALLOY: Do more work.

COACH JAMISON: Well, look, you did one hell of a number on her. . . .

PHILIP MALLOY: I mean, I'm not even in her class anymore. She must have kicked me out.

COACH JAMISON: They put you in another class?

PHILIP MALLOY: Yeah, but I was trying to get some extra work. . . . If I could stay in her class I—

COACH JAMISON: Philip, you want my advice?

PHILIP MALLOY: I tried—

COACH JAMISON: I'm always telling you guys—it's what sports is all about—a rule is a rule—to get along you have to play along. Know what I'm saying?

PHILIP MALLOY: What about my running with the team?

COACH JAMISON: Look, Philip, you did a number on Miss Narwin. Didn't I tell you —right from the start— you were way off base? She's a good person. You have to be a team player. Haven't you heard me say that? So you can't just come around now and start asking me for things. It just doesn't work that way. Look, Phil, I've got a practice. And look, by next year this'll all be over. I sure hope so.

**DR. DOANE:** Would you like a cup of coffee?

**MISS NARWIN:** My nerves are too tight as it is.

**DR. DOANE:** It's astonishing. . . . Did I tell you, I had another call from a TV reporter—

**MISS NARWIN:** No. Absolutely not.

**DR. DOANE:** I don't blame you.

**MISS NARWIN:** You wanted to see me. . . .

**DR. DOANE:** Just that some good has come out of all this. . . .

**MISS NARWIN:** That would be nice. What is it?

**DR. DOANE:** Peg, do you remember you put in an application for funds? Some kind of refresher course, English teaching. I'm not sure what. For the summer.

**MISS NARWIN:** Vaguely.

**DR. DOANE:** I talked to Al Seymour and—

**MISS NARWIN:** Don't mention him to me. That statement—

**DR. DOANE:** As a way of showing his support, he managed to find some money, and you can take that special course. . . .

**MISS NARWIN:** Well, that is nice.

DR. DOANE: We'll expedite the application.

MISS NARWIN: I'm very grateful.

DR. DOANE: There is only one thing. . . .

MISS NARWIN: The deadline?

DR. DOANE: No, it's not that. Peg, knowing how upsetting this all is, the superintendent wants you to take the rest of the term off.

MISS NARWIN: What?

DR. DOANE: The rest of the term.

MISS NARWIN: But . . .

DR. DOANE: Well, Al knows, because I told him, how upsetting all this is to you, and . . . Take the time off, full pay, of course, and then, take that course, and you'll come back fall term . . . and, well, things will be fine. It's very kind of him.

MISS NARWIN: In other words, he wants me to leave.

DR. DOANE: No. No. You've misunderstood. Truly, Peg. Only as a way of getting out from the pressure. I mean, all these telegrams. Calls. It would be administrative leave. You'll lose no time on your pension. As I said, full-time. With pay. You could be with your sister. . . . A sabbatical. You've never had one.

MISS NARWIN: No.

DR. DOANE: Peg, you have to see it from his, our side. . . .

MISS NARWIN: Aren't we on the same side?

DR. DOANE: That's not the point.

MISS NARWIN: What *is* the point?

DR. DOANE: Peg, Al is deeply worried about our budget.

---

**6:30 P.M.**
**Conversation**
**between Philip Malloy's Parents**

---

MR. MALLOY: Hey, where's Philip?

MRS. MALLOY: Up in his room.

MR. MALLOY: These telegrams. Incredible.

MRS. MALLOY: He's very upset.

MR. MALLOY: About the telegrams?

MRS. MALLOY: Something at school.

MR. MALLOY: That teacher again?

MRS. MALLOY: He wouldn't say. When he came home, I don't think he even looked at that stack. He doesn't seem very happy. He wouldn't talk about it.

MR. MALLOY: Weird.

MRS. MALLOY: I almost thought he was going to start crying.

MR. MALLOY: *Crying?*

MRS. MALLOY: Maybe you could talk to him.

MR. MALLOY: Sure.

MRS. MALLOY: Dinner will be ready in twenty minutes.

MR. MALLOY: I'll talk to him.

MRS. MALLOY: Hon!

MR. MALLOY: What?

MRS. MALLOY: My sister called.

MR. MALLOY: From Conover?

MRS. MALLOY: She said Philip could go to school in their district.

MR. MALLOY: That's absurd!

MRS. MALLOY: Maybe it isn't. Maybe this is too much.

MR. MALLOY: Susan . . .

MRS. MALLOY: Just a thought.

---

**6:45 P.M.**
**Phone Conversation**
**between Margaret Narwin and Her Sister,**
**Anita Wigham**

---

ANITA WIGHAM: Peg, I am shocked!

MISS NARWIN: Well, you can imagine how I felt. The dishonesty of it! And from Gertrude of all people. I still find it impossible to believe.

ANITA WIGHAM: But what are you going to do?

MISS NARWIN: Anita, I don't know. I truly don't know.

---

**6:50 P.M.**
**Conversation**
**between Philip Malloy and His Father**

---

MR. MALLOY: Philip, I want you to open the door so we can talk.

PHILIP MALLOY: I don't want to talk.

MR. MALLOY: What happened in school?

PHILIP MALLOY: Nothing.

MR. MALLOY: Look, dinner will be ready in five minutes.

PHILIP MALLOY: I'm not hungry.

MR. MALLOY: Then what are you going to do?

PHILIP MALLOY: I don't know.

---

**8:30 P.M.**
**From a Speech**
**Delivered by Ted Griffen**
**to a Meeting of the**
**Harrison Downtown Association**

---

MR. GRIFFEN: That I can be a forceful, productive member of the board is clear. It was I who made public this sad story regarding a boy who was removed from class merely because of his desire to express his patriotism. Even though I am not yet a member of the board, I was able to meet with Superintendent Seymour—who has, I assure you, my deepest respect—and discuss in a calm, rational fashion what might be done. When it became clear that the problem was not with school policy itself, but the misguided judgment of a particular teacher—a teacher out of touch with Harrison values—a solution was worked out that is equitable to all—and preserves the good name of our community. The boy is back in class, where he belongs and wants to be. The teacher in question will get a needed refresher course in our values and return to her duties next year better able to teach.

Our community will support just these kinds of productive compromises. And therefore I urge all of you, on April fifth, to support the school budget proposal set before the voters. It is a thoughtful budget. Let me make this perfectly clear. The budget is fiscally prudent, and I, for one, support it.

---

**8:50 P.M.**
**From the Diary of Philip Malloy**

---

Things stink. And it's all so unfair. Nobody takes my side. They all think Narwin's great. Nobody pays any attention to what she did to me. Coach Jamison won't let me on the team.

I hate that school.

---

**9:30 P.M.**
**Phone Conversation**
**between Margaret Narwin**
**and Robert Duval, Reporter**

---

MISS NARWIN: I really don't wish to talk about it.

MR. DUVAL: Ma'am, Miss Narwin, it seems to me, from what I've come to understand about you and what happened, that the original story does not make a great deal of sense. For instance, at one point, Dr. Doane—your principal—told me you were one of the district's best teachers.

MISS NARWIN: Did she?

MR. DUVAL: Yes, ma'am. She did.

MISS NARWIN: I'm not so sure she would still say so.

MR. DUVAL: What do you mean?

MISS NARWIN: Mr. Duval . . . I . . .

MR. DUVAL: Miss Narwin, I am truly interested in getting out your story. It's been awfully one-sided.

MISS NARWIN: That's certainly true. People seem to believe that this boy is . . . rather special. Nobody seems to want to pay any attention to what actually happened. I've been asked to resign.

MR. DUVAL: By whom?

MISS NARWIN: The school. The district.

MR. DUVAL: Miss Narwin, I'm prepared to fly out and talk to you. I really do think there is something important here. I'd like to get it out to the public. Miss Narwin?

MISS NARWIN: Very well. Come along. I'll talk to you.

# Chapter 17

## Wednesday, April 4

---

**7:20 A.M.**
**Phone Conversation**
**between Margaret Narwin**
**and Dr. Gertrude Doane**

---

DR. DOANE: Yes, Peg?

MISS NARWIN: I won't be coming in today.

DR. DOANE: Oh.

MISS NARWIN: I'm too exhausted.

DR. DOANE: I think that's wise.

MISS NARWIN: I need time to think.

DR. DOANE: You do that. No problem here. We'll get a substitute.

---

**7:30 A.M.**
**Conversation**
**between Philip Malloy and His Parents**
**at Breakfast**

---

PHILIP MALLOY: No way I'm going to school.

MR. MALLOY: Why?

PHILIP MALLOY: I just won't.

MRS. MALLOY: Philip, you must tell us. Has that teacher done something else?

PHILIP MALLOY: I'm not in her classes anymore.

MR. MALLOY: But . . . Look at all these telegrams. Everybody says you did the right thing.

PHILIP MALLOY: I'm not going.

MR. MALLOY: Philip, you must go.

PHILIP MALLOY: I'll go to another school. You said there was a private school.

MRS. MALLOY: But . . .

MR. MALLOY: Oh, sure! Go to private school! The only money we've got is the money we've been putting aside for your college.

PHILIP MALLOY: I could go up to Aunt Becky's. We could move.

MR. MALLOY: That's ridiculous. Look, it's clear *something* has happened. If we don't know, how can we help you?

PHILIP MALLOY: The kids hate me!

MR. MALLOY: Why?

PHILIP MALLOY: I'm not going.

MR. MALLOY: Philip, you will go!

**7:40 A.M.**
**Conversation**
**between Philip Malloy and Ken Barchet**
**on the Way to the School Bus**

PHILIP MALLOY: What's happening?

KEN BARCHET: Nothing. What's with you? I thought maybe you weren't going to school.

PHILIP MALLOY: My folks , . .

KEN BARCHET: Did you hear what Allison and Todd were planning to do?

PHILIP MALLOY: No, what?

KEN BARCHET: They want to get a petition going to get you to say you were wrong.

PHILIP MALLOY: No way.

KEN BARCHET: And you know who gave them the idea?

PHILIP MALLOY: No,

KEN BARCHET: Coach Jamison.

PHILIP MALLOY: You kidding?

KEN BARCHET: That's what Brian told me. Want me to start another petition to get Narwin to apologize? Or we could get you to sing together. Be boss.

PHILIP MALLOY: Would you stop bugging me!

KEN BARCHET: Hey, man, can't you take a joke?

PHILIP MALLOY: Forget it!

KEN BARCHET: Hey! Come on, Phil. Where you going? I was just kidding!

PHILIP MALLOY: Just want you to know I'm home.

MRS. MALLOY: *Home?* Why?

PHILIP MALLOY: I told you: I'm not going to school. Not that school.

MRS. MALLOY: Well . . . stay home today. That's okay. We'll talk it out when I get home.

PHILIP MALLOY: Just don't tell Dad, will you?

MRS. MALLOY: Okay.

MRS. MALLOY: Ben, but he refuses to go back!

MR. MALLOY: I've never heard of anything so crazy. He won! But he acts as if he's lost.

MRS. MALLOY: He says he'll just wait till we're out of the house and then come home.

MR. MALLOY: Of all . . .

MRS. MALLOY: He has to go to some school.

MR. MALLOY: Right . . .

MRS. MALLOY: I'm going to call Washington Academy.

MR. MALLOY: That's his college money!

**MRS. MALLOY:** Or should I call my sister?

---

### 12:30 P.M.
### Conversation
### between Margaret Narwin
### and Robert Duval, Reporter

---

**MR. DUVAL:** Miss Narwin, how do you see what has happened? A summary.

**MISS NARWIN:** I think and I think. And—that boy—Philip Malloy—for reasons I'll never learn— decided to insult me, his classmates, and, as far as that goes, the national anthem. Yes, I sent him from my room. But it wasn't I who sent him home. I objected to that. Objected strongly. Yet I've been blamed for his suspension. It's I who has been asked to resign.

**MR. DUVAL:** Resign?

**MISS NARWIN:** They say it's a leave. But Mr. Duval, I'm not stupid. Naïve perhaps. But not stupid. I should be in school right this moment, teaching my students. Teaching them the literature that I love. That they desperately need. Who else will give it to them? But where am I? I'm home—surrounded by letters, and telegrams too—from people, perfect strangers who know nothing about me, who hate me. The post office brought a sack of letters this morning. That's why I'm talking to you. I'm trying to defend myself.

Mr. Duval, as I see it, I have been working— working hard—as a teacher for twenty years. I've been a good teacher. Ask my principal if that's not so. Do you know, she was once my student.

MR. DUVAL: Is that right?

MISS NARWIN: Oh, yes. One of the brightest. But did *anyone*—anyone outside—ever stop and notice those years of good teaching—did they write a story about *that?* No. That's not what people are interested in. Do you know—I feel like I've been mugged. Assaulted.

MR. DUVAL: By whom?

MISS NARWIN: I wish I knew.

MR. DUVAL: Ma'am, do you think there's some reason that this has happened?

MISS NARWIN: Reason? Mr. Duval, I keep wishing there was a reason. No, no reason at all.

MR. DUVAL: Do you have any idea what you will do about it?

MISS NARWIN: I told you, I'm thinking of resigning.

# Chapter 18

Friday, April 6

HARRISON SCHOOL ELECTIONS

Final results, vote for school budget:
In Favor: 645
Against: 1,784
*Budget Defeated*

The following were elected to the Harrison
School Board for three-year terms:
Susan Eagleton
Ted Griffen
Gloria Haviland
Ernest Johnson
Crawford Wright

Percentage of eligible voters casting ballots:
22%

MISS NARWIN: Mr. Duval?

MR. DUVAL: Speaking.

MISS NARWIN: This is Margaret Narwin, from Harrison.

MR. DUVAL: Oh, yes, Miss Narwin. How are you, ma'am?

MISS NARWIN: I'm fine. I wanted to ask you if you published that story—that story that you interviewed me for.

MR. DUVAL: Oh, right. Well, I certainly wrote it. And it has been filed, It was a pretty good story. All set to go too. But then South America . . . that situation . . . There's no room.

MISS NARWIN: Then you won't print it?

MR. DUVAL: Well, it's possible. But I'd be less than candid with you if I said it will appear. With so much happening . . .

MISS NARWIN: I see.

MR. DUVAL: I am sorry. I'm sure you would have liked to see it in print. . . .

MISS NARWIN: Yes. . . .

MR. DUVAL: Did you decide what to do, ma'am?

MISS NARWIN: I'm . . . I'm calling from the airport now. I'm going to Florida. To be with my sister. And her husband.

MR. DUVAL: You've resigned, then.

MISS NARWIN: I need some time to think. . . .

MR. DUVAL: Yes, I understand. And I—excuse me, I'm being called. . . .

# Chapter 19

## Monday, April 9

---

**8:25 A.M.**
**Conversation**
**between Philip Malloy**
**and George Brookover,**
**Principal of Washington Academy**

---

**GEORGE BROOKOVER:** Philip, I just wanted to tell you that we're very pleased to have you at Washington Academy. We do know a good bit about you. You're pretty famous.

**PHILIP MALLOY:** Yes, sir.

**GEORGE BROOKOVER:** We like what we hear. Anyway, we're all pretty much a family at Washington. I'm sure you'll make new friends.

**PHILIP MALLOY:** Yes, sir.

**GEORGE BROOKOVER:** You'll be in Miss Rooney's class. You'll find her a good teacher. I'm sure you'll do just fine. Have you any interest in sports?

**PHILIP MALLOY:** Track.

**GEORGE BROOKOVER:** Well, we don't have a track team here at Washington. There's never been enough interest. But now that you're here, maybe there can be. Your dad says you're a crackerjack runner. We do have soccer. You could do a lot of running there. Think that might interest you?

PHILIP MALLOY: I don't know.

GEORGE BROOKOVER: Okay. Let me take you on down to class now. Should be just getting under way.

---

**8:30 A.M.**
**Discussion**
**in Miss Rooney's Homeroom Class,**
**Washington Academy**

---

MISS ROONEY: Class, this is Philip Malloy, who has just joined our school. Philip, you can sit right over there. We were about to begin. In fact, we usually begin by singing the national anthem. Maybe you'd like to lead us in that? Philip? Philip, what's the matter? Why are you crying?

PHILIP MALLOY: I don't know the words.

# RELATED READINGS

# honesty

## by Don Marquis

*In the 1930s a humorist named Don
Marquis published short poems and letters
that he claimed had been written by a
cockroach named archy. He said these
messages were in his typewriter every
morning—composed as the little
cockroach jumped from key to key. How
well do you think this cockroach's opinion
of honesty fits humans?*

honesty is a good
thing but
it is not profitable to
its possessor
5    unless it is
kept under control
if you are not
honest at all
everybody hates you
10   and if you are
absolutely honest
you get martyred.

# A Nice Old-Fashioned Romance, With Love Lyrics and Everything

by William Saroyan

*What kind of disasters can happen when no one believes that you are telling the truth?*

My cousin Arak was a year and a half younger than me, round-faced, dark, and exceptionally elegant in manners. It was no pretense with him. His manners were just naturally that way, just as my manners were bad from the beginning. Where Arak would get around any sort of complication at school with a bland smile that showed his front upper teeth, separated, and melted the heart of stone of our teacher, Miss Daffney, I would go to the core of the complication and with noise and vigor prove that Miss Daffney or somebody else was the culprit, not me, and if need be, I would carry the case to the Supreme Court and prove my innocence.

I usually got sent to the office. In some cases I would get a strapping for debating the case in the office against Mr. Derringer, our principal, who was no earthly good at debates. The minute I got him cornered he got out his strap.

Arak was different; he didn't care to fight for justice. He wasn't anywhere near as bright as me, but even though he was a year and a half younger than me, he was in the same grade. That wouldn't be so bad if the grade wasn't the fifth. I usually won all my arguments with my teachers, but instead of being glad to get rid of me they refused to promote me, in the hope, I believe, of winning the following semester's arguments and getting even. That's how it happened that I came to be the oldest pupil in the fifth grade.

One day Miss Daffney tried to tell the world I was the author of the poem on the blackboard that said she was in love with Mr. Derringer, and ugly. The author of the poem was my cousin Arak, not me. Any poem I wrote wouldn't be about Miss Daffney, it would be about something worthwhile. Nevertheless, without mentioning any names, but with a ruler in her hand, Miss Daffney stood beside my desk and said, I am going to find out who is responsible for this horrible outrage on the blackboard and see that he is properly punished.

*He?* I said. How do you know it's a boy and not a girl?

Miss Daffney whacked me on the knuckles of my right hand. I jumped out of my seat and said, You can't go around whacking me on the knuckles. I'll report this.

Sit down, Miss Daffney said.

I did. She had me by the right ear, which was getting out of shape from being grabbed hold of by Miss Daffney and other teachers.

I sat down and quietly, almost inaudibly, said, You'll hear about this.

Hold your tongue, Miss Daffney said, and although I was sore as the devil, I stuck out my tongue and held it, while the little Mexican, Japanese, Armenian, Greek, Italian, Portuguese, and other American boys and girls in the class, who looked to me for comedy, roared with laughter. Miss Daffney came down on my hand with the ruler, but this time the ruler grazed my nose. This to me was particularly insulting, inasmuch as my nose then, as now, was large. A small nose would not have been grazed, and I took Miss Daffney's whack as a subtle comment on the size of my nose.

I put my bruised hand over my hurt nose and again rose to my feet.

You told me to hold my tongue, I said, insisting that I had done no evil, had merely carried out her instructions, and was therefore innocent, utterly undeserving of the whacked hand and the grazed nose.

You be good now, Miss Daffney said. I won't stand any more of your nonsense.

I took my hand away from my nose and began to be good. I smiled like a boy bringing her a red apple. My audience roared with laughter and Miss Daffney dropped the ruler, reached for me, fell over the desk, got up, and began to chase me around the room.

There I go again, I kept saying to myself while Miss Daffney chased me around the room. There I go again getting in a mess like this that's sure to end in murder, while my cousin Arak, who is the guilty one, sits there and smiles. There's no justice anywhere.

When Miss Daffney finally caught me, as I knew she would unless I wanted even more severe punishment from Mr. Derringer, there was a sort of free-for-all during which she tried to gouge my eyes out, pull off my ears, fingers, and arms, and I, by argument, tried to keep her sweet and lady-like.

When she was exhausted, I went back to my seat, and the original crime of the day was taken up again: Who was the author of the love lyric on the blackboard?

Miss Daffney straightened her hair and her clothes, got her breath, demanded and got silence, and after several moments of peace during which the ticking of the clock was heard, she began to speak.

I am going to ask each of you by name if you wrote this awful—poem—on the blackboard and I shall expect you to tell the truth. If you lie, I shall find out anyway and your punishment will be all the worse.

She began to ask each of the boys and girls if they'd written the poem and of course they hadn't. Then she asked my cousin Arak and he also said he hadn't. Then she asked me and I said I hadn't, which was the truth.

You go to the office, she said. You liar.

I didn't write any poem on any blackboard, I said. And I'm not a liar.

Mr. Derringer received me with no delight. Two minutes later Susie Kokomoto arrived from our class with a message describing my crime. In fact, quoting it. Mr. Derringer read the message, made six or seven faces, smiled, snapped his suspenders, coughed and said, What made you write this little poem?

I didn't, I said.

Naturally, he said, you'd say you didn't, but why did you?

I *didn't* write it, I said.

Now don't be headstrong, Mr. Derringer said. That's a rather alarming rumor to be spreading. How do you *know* Miss Daffney's in love with me?

*Is she?* I said.

Well, Mr. Derringer said, that's what it says here. What gave you that impression? Have you noticed her looking at me with admiration or something?

I haven't noticed her looking at you with anything, I said. Are *you* in love with *her* or something?

That remains to be seen, Mr. Derringer said. It isn't a bad poem, up to a point. Do you really regard Miss Daffney as ugly?

I didn't write the poem, I said. I can prove it. I don't write that way.

You mean your handwriting isn't like the handwriting on the blackboard? Mr. Derringer said.

Yes, I said, and I don't write that kind of poetry either.

You *admit* writing poetry? Mr. Derringer said.

I write poetry, I said, but not *that* kind of poetry.

A rumor like that, Mr. Derringer said. I hope you know what you're about.

Well, I said, all I know is I didn't write it.

Personally, Mr. Derringer said, I think Miss Daffney is not only not ugly, but on the contrary attractive.

Well, that's all right, I said. The only thing I want is not to get into a lot of trouble over something I didn't do.

You *could* have written that poem, Mr. Derringer said.

Not *that* one, I said. I could have written a good one.

What do you mean, *good?* Mr. Derringer said. Beautiful? Or insulting?

I mean beautiful, I said, only it wouldn't be about Miss Daffney.

Up to this point, Mr. Derringer said, I was willing to entertain doubts as to your being the author of the poem, but no longer. I am convinced you wrote it.

Therefore I must punish you.

I got up and started to debate.

You give me a strapping for something I didn't do, I said, and you'll hear about it.

So he gave me a strapping and *the whole school* heard about it. I went back to class limping. The poem had been erased. All was well again. The culprit had been duly punished, the poem effaced, and order reestablished in the fifth grade. My cousin Arak sat quietly admiring Alice Bovard's brown curls.

First thing during recess I knocked him down and sat on him.

I got a strapping for that, I said, so don't write any more of them.

The next morning, however, there was another love lyric on the blackboard in my cousin Arak's unmistakable hand, and in his unmistakable style, and once again Miss Daffney wanted to weed out the culprit and have him punished. When I came into the room and saw the poem and the lay of the land I immediately began to object. My cousin Arak was going too far. In Armenian I began to swear at him. He, however, had become stone deaf, and Miss Daffney believed my talk was for her. Here, here, she said.

All I've got to say is I didn't write that poem, I said. And I didn't write yesterday's either. If I get into any more trouble on account of these poems, somebody's going to hear about it.

Sit down, Miss Daffney said.

After the roll call, Miss Daffney filled a whole sheet of paper with writing, including the new poem, and ordered me to take the message to the office.

Why *me?* I said. I didn't write the poem.

Do as you're told, Miss Daffney said.

I went to her desk, put out my hand to take the

note, Miss Daffney gave it a whack, I jumped back three feet and shouted, I'm not going to be carrying love-letters for you.

This just naturally was the limit. There was a limit to everything. Miss Daffney leaped at me. I in turn was so sore at my cousin Arak that I turned around and jumped on him. He pretended to be very innocent, and offered no resistance. He was very deft, though, and instead of getting the worst of it, he got the least, while I fell all over the floor until Miss Daffney caught up with me. After that it was all her fight. When I got to the office with the message, I had scratches and bruises all over my face and hands, and the love-letter from Miss Daffney to Mr. Derringer was crumpled and in places torn.

What's been keeping you? Mr. Derringer said. Here, let me see that message. What mischief have you been up to now?

He took the message, unfolded it, smoothed it out on his desk, and read it very slowly. He read it three or four times. He was delighted, and, as far as I could tell, in love. He turned with a huge smile on his face and was about to reprimand me again for saying that Miss Daffney was ugly.

I didn't write the poem, I said. I didn't write yesterday's either. All I want is a chance to get myself a little education and live and let live.

Now, now, Mr. Derringer said.

He was quite pleased.

If you're in love with her, I said, that's your affair, but leave me out of it.

All I say is you could be a little more gracious about Miss Daffney's appearance, Mr. Derringer said. If she seems plain to you, perhaps she doesn't seem plain to someone else.

I was disgusted. It was just no use.

All right, I said. Tomorrow I'll be gracious.

Now that's better, Mr. Derringer said. Of course I must punish you.

He reached for the lower drawer of his desk where the strap was.

Oh, no, I said. If you punish me, then I won't be gracious.

Well, what about today's poem? Mr. Derringer said. I've got to punish you for that. Tomorrow's will be another story.

No, I said. Nothing doing.

Oh, all right, Mr. Derringer said, but see that you're gracious.

I will, I said. Can I go back now?

Yes, he said. Yes. Let me think this over.

I began to leave the office.

Wait a minute, he said. Everybody'll know something fishy's going on somewhere unless they hear you howl. Better come back here and howl ten times, and then go back.

How? I said. I can't howl unless I'm hurt.

Oh, sure you can, Mr. Derringer said. Just give out a big painful howl. You can do it.

I don't think I can, I said.

I'll hit this chair ten times with the strap, Mr. Derringer said, and you howl.

Do you think it'll work? I said.

Of course it'll work, he said. Come on.

Mr. Derringer hit the chair with the strap and I tried to howl the way I had howled yesterday, but it didn't sound real. It sounded fishy, somewhere.

We were going along that way when Miss Daffney herself came into the office, only we didn't know she'd come in, on account of the noise.

On the tenth one I turned to Mr. Derringer and said, That's ten.

Then I saw Miss Daffney. She was aghast and mouth-agape.

Just a few more, son, Mr. Derringer said, for good measure.

Before I could tell him Miss Daffney was in the office, he was whacking the chair and I was howling.

It was disgusting.

Miss Daffney coughed and Mr. Derringer turned and saw her—his beloved.

Miss Daffney didn't speak. She *couldn't*. Mr. Derringer smiled. He was very embarrassed and began swinging the strap around.

I'm punishing the boy, he said.

I understand, Miss Daffney said.

She didn't either. Not altogether anyway.

I'll not have any pupil of this school being impertinent, Mr. Derringer said.

He was madly in love with her and was swinging the strap around and trying to put over a little personality. Miss Daffney, however, just didn't think very much of his punishing the boy by hitting a chair, while the boy howled, the man and the boy together making a mockery of justice and true love. She gave him a very dirty look.

Oh! Mr. Derringer said. You mean about my hitting the chair? We were just rehearsing, weren't we, son?

*No, we weren't,* I said.

Miss Daffney, infuriated, turned and fled, and Mr. Derringer sat down.

Now look what you've done, he said.

Well, I said, if you're going to have a romance with her, have it, but don't mess me up in it.

Well, Mr. Derringer said, I guess that's that. He was a very sad man.

All right, he said, go back to your class.

I want you to know I didn't write them poems, I said.

That's got nothing to do with it, Mr. Derringer said.

I thought you might want to know, I said.

It's too late now, he said. She'll never admire me any more.

Why don't you write a poem to her yourself? I said.

*I can't write poems,* Mr. Derringer said.

Well, I said, figure it out some way.

When I went back to class Miss Daffney was very polite. So was I. She knew I knew and she knew if she got funny I'd either ruin the romance or make her marry him, so she was very friendly. In two weeks school closed and when school opened again Miss Daffney didn't show up. Either Mr. Derringer didn't write her a poem, or did and it was no good; or he didn't tell her he loved her, or did and she didn't care; or else he proposed to her and she turned him down, *because I knew,* and got herself transferred to another school so she could get over her broken heart.

Something like that.

# *from* Journey to Washington

## by Daniel Inouye

*Daniel Inouye, elected as the state of Hawaii's first U.S. Senator in 1963, is of Japanese descent. As a teenager his parents wanted him to be aware of his ethnic heritage, but there was no question in Inouye's mind that he was first and foremost an American.*

I didn't wear shoes regularly until I was in high school—none of us *nisei* kids did—and it was as much a matter of comfort as money. After all, this was Hawaii, a truly blessed place for a boy to grow up in.

We were a trial to our teachers, I'm sure. Many of them were *haoles* from the Mainland, properly reared and educated young ladies, and they must have been disconcerted, to say the least, to be suddenly confronted with a ragtag crew of barefooted, sport-shirted kids whose English was liberally larded with Japanese, Chinese, Hawaiian and some exotic combinations of each. But they were a wonderfully dedicated group and they did their best to make educated Americans out of us young savages. And even more important, they accepted us on our own terms—they didn't despair over us, or patronize us, or slough us off as inferiors and hopeless delinquents. They treated us as exactly what we were, a bunch of kids from poor homes with hard-working parents, with a sort of built-in eagerness to become part of the mainstream of American life, and there is no way in which I can adequately express my thanks to them.

I loved school. Each day brought its own separate reward and learning became a constantly intriguing challenge. Of course when you're a boy there is always a danger of being tagged a bookworm and, in natural consequence, a sissy-pants. And so I was careful not to be caught studying or doing more homework than was absolutely necessary, and I warily cultivated a manner of dress and classroom manner that, even by our group's casual standard, was pretty flamboyant.

By this time we had returned to Coyne Street, in an area officially known as Bingham Tract but more readily recognizable by its popular name: Chinese Hollywood. Here Chinese families clustered together, and here came aspiring Americans from China with every new ship bound east from the Orient. The Inouyes were one of only two Japanese families in Bingham and, perhaps inevitably, we were soon virtually adopted by our sweet-natured neighbors. To this day I am known by our old neighbors as Ah-Danny-Jai, affectionate Chinese for little Danny.

As for me, I acquired a highly-cultivated taste for Chinese delicacies, not the least of which was dried water beetles. When these were roasted, the tails could be pulled from the body and made a delicious snack, like peanuts. One day, hungry as usual, I took a whole bagful of these morsels to school with me and whiled away the afternoon cracking them and stuffing the tasty tails into my mouth. So long as there was activity in the classroom I was safe, the teacher couldn't hear me and I took care that she didn't see me. But toward the end of the day, with all of us hushed in assigned study, the sharp crack of a beetle back sounded through the silent room like a rifle shot. Miss Dolton, who was blond and beautiful, looked up and I looked down. Miss Dolton looked down and—CRACK!—went another beetle.

"Dan!"

"Gmmm?" I mumbled, my mouth stuffed with tails.

"Are you *eating* something?"

I nodded, trying to express an apology with my eyes alone.

"Well!" said the proper young lady indignantly. "You know the rule about eating in class. Now you may bring whatever it is you have there up to me and I will take my share and pass it around to the class."

Now, as you can see, this was truly punishment to fit the crime—forcing any of us kids to give up food was like shredding a tobacco addict's last cigarette. Crushed and contrite, and still unable to speak a word in my defense, I carried my precious bag up front and deposited it on Miss Dolton's desk. Whereupon she righteously reached in, produced a beetle and, on the verge of popping it into her mouth, caught sight of what she was holding and delivered herself of a shriek that, they say, was heard on the far side of Diamond Head. Into the wastebasket went my bag—punishment enough!— and back to my seat I marched, directed by Miss Dolton's quivering finger. Years later, when I went back to see her, we had many laughs over my school days. But when I brought up the matter of the Chinese water beetles, the same look of dread crossed her face, and she said, "Oh, Dan, how could you!"

The trouble I got into at Japanese language school was somewhat more serious and crystallized for me, once and for all, the matter of who I was and where in this cultural melting pot I was headed. Most of my contemporaries quit at the end of the tenth year, by which time they had a fair grounding in Japanese history and tradition. In deference to my grand-parents, I suppose, I was enrolled for the eleventh grade and sat through excruciatingly long afternoons listening to lectures on the sacredness of the royal family and being admonished to preserve the centuries-old customs of my people. Then, all in one cataclysmic afternoon, I unburdened myself of my smoldering resentment and, in consequence, was flung bodily from the classroom, never to return.

The year was 1939 and already times had turned tense in the Far East. The Japanese government was in the iron grip of fanatic warlords and the Imperial Army was waging aggressive war in China and menacing all of Southeast Asia. Day after day, the priest who taught us ethics and Japanese history hammered away at the divine prerogatives of the Emperor, and at the grand destiny that called on the Japanese people to extend their sway over the yellow race, and on the madness that was inducing the American government to oppose them. He would tilt his menacing crew-cut skull at us and solemnly proclaim, "You must remember that only a trick of fate has brought you so far from your homeland, but there must be no question of your loyalty. When Japan calls, you must know that it is Japanese blood that flows in your veins."

I had heard his jingoistic little speeches so many times that I suppose they no longer really registered on me. He was an old man, to be respected for his station, but when he began spouting nonsense I could easily tune him out. But one day he shifted his scorn to the Bible and I reacted by instinct—and violently. He had been discussing the inadequacy of

Christianity compared to Shintoism, the state religion of Japan, and already my hackles were up. Then he favored us with an elaborate grin and, mockery dripping from his every word, he said, "I give you the Bible itself as the best evidence of this Christian foolishness. Their God made the world in seven days, it says. Ha! Then he made a man and from a rib of that man—a rib, mark you!—he made a woman. Ha! Anyone with only part of a brain can see that this is the wildest nonsense!"

I never realized that I was on my feet and shouting until I saw the grin on his face twist, first into astonishment, and then into fury. Then my words echoed in my head:

"That's not right! That's not fair! I am a Christian, a lot of us here are, and you mustn't talk that way! I respect your faith. You must respect mine."

"How dare you!" he roared

"I do. I do dare! You have no right to make fun of my beliefs."

"You are a Japanese! You will believe what I . . ."

"I am an American!"

He flinched, exactly as though I had struck him. With a single compulsive jerk, he threw the book he had been holding through the open window, and we watched the pages flutter in the wind for a moment. Then he started toward me, and the class watched in silent terror, and his face was black as a thunderhead and his mouth worked violently as he cried, "You are a Japanese!" Now his fingers clutched at my open collar and he was shaking me back and forth "Say it!" he screamed into my face. "You are a Japanese!"

And barely able to bring my voice up out of my tortured throat, I muttered, "I—am—an—American."

With that, he lifted me from my feet and

half-dragged, half-carried me to the door, and he threw me with full force into the schoolyard. "You are a faithless dog!" he screamed, and slammed the door closed.

Dazed and trembling, I stumbled to my feet. My trousers were torn and one knee was scraped and bleeding. Crazily, my first thought was how to hide this from my mother. But I had only taken a few steps toward home when I realized that I didn't want to hide it. I had had all I could take of that Japanese teacher and if it took this catastrophe—and the punishment I was sure to get for it—to free me, well, so be it.

But, of course, I had underestimated my mother again. She took one look at my tattered pants and the mutinous expression I wore, and she demanded the whole story. And I told it to her, and all the time I spoke she was washing and bandaging my skinned knee, so that I could not see her face and could not gauge how she was reacting to this great crisis in my life. But when I was all finished, she got to her feet and said, "Come, we are going back there."

This was something more than I had bargained for. Maybe I had used up my day's supply of bravery, but the fact is that I had no desire to face the priest's wrath again. "Mama," I began hesitantly . . .

She shushed me. "You have nothing to fear or to be ashamed of," she said crisply. "But there is a matter of honor to be settled."

Nor did she waste any time on the teacher. Instead, she went directly to the office of the principal, a gentle and distinguished Japanese. And Mother stood before his desk, a tiny figure whose massive indignation strengthened her words, and she told him exactly what happened. "I do not send him here to become a Shintoist or a samurai. I want him to learn the language and traditions of his ancestors, but we are Americans and shall always remain so."

Amazingly, he nodded his agreement. He would speak to the priest, he assured my mother. There would be no more such authoritarian teaching, and I could return to my class without fear of retribution.

"That is up to Ken," my mother said looking straight at me and using, as she almost always did, my Japanese name. "He is old enough now to decide this for himself."

And I said, "I don't want to go back. I've learned enough about the old ways." My mother thanked the principal for hearing her out, and we left, and for the first time, I suppose, I knew what it was to *feel* like an American. . . .

# For LB, 1943–1993

by Cecil Morris

*Some teachers stay in their students'*
*memories for a lifetime. Do you think*
*anyone in Miss Narwin's classes might*
*think she was something like LB?*

My high school English teacher seemed
    younger
than her years, her skin still slate smooth,
    her eyes
intense as freshly sharpened pencils, her
mind as nimble as typist's fingers. Still
5    she died, not waking from one night's
    slumber,
slipping gentle into that good night we
all must face. I saw her three days before,
heard her hearty laugh—from the
diaphragm—
laughed myself at the bawdy tale she told
10   and took three books she said I had to read.

Two friends found her in her bed, a book
beside her, as firm in her repose
as she had been in life, her face her death
    mask
ready for the teacher's rest, that narrow
15  apse off Poet's Corner at Westminster
where she made the rubbing she brought for
    us

to see and touch. They said, though pale and
    still,
she looked as if caught in some happy
    thought,
as if crossing over some well-loved page
20    and finding a phrase put just right.

Tonight, with her books stacked beside my
    bed,
I recall how she swelled like air or light
to fill her class until we inhaled words
with every breath. Words words words she
    told us
25    words are everything. There's no chill so
    cold
that words can't warm it. She gave us new
    words—
amanuensis, amaranth, ambiv-
alent—and let us play with them. Each week
she unwrapped new authors—from Chaucer
    to
30    Auden—and let us warm ourselves with
    them.

She taught me the magic that words can do,
spoke the abracadabra that has shaped
my life, and proves tonight that words spoke
    right
transcend the moment of their speaking.

# The Catbird Seat

by James Thurber

*Have you ever known anyone who looks incapable of doing anything wrong? Read this story to find out how somebody uses this quality to manipulate others.*

Mr. Martin bought the pack of Camels on Monday night in the most crowded cigar store on Broadway. It was theater time and seven or eight men were buying cigarettes. The clerk didn't even glance at Mr. Martin, who put the pack in his overcoat pocket and went out. If any of the staff at F & S had seen him buy the cigarettes, they would have been astonished, for it was generally known that Mr. Martin did not smoke, and never had. No one saw him.

It was just a week to the day since Mr. Martin had decided to rub out Mrs. Ulgine Barrows. The term "rub out" pleased him because it suggested nothing more than the correction of an error—in this case an error of Mr. Fitweiler. Mr. Martin had spent each night of the past week working out his plan and examining it. As he walked home now he went over it again. For the hundredth time he resented the element of imprecision, the margin of guesswork that entered into the business. The project as he had worked it out was casual and bold, the risks were considerable. Something might go wrong anywhere along the line. And therein lay the cunning of his scheme. No one would ever see in it the cautious, painstaking hand of Erwin Martin, head of the filing department at F & S, of whom Mr. Fitweiler had once said, "Man is fallible but Martin isn't." No one would see his hand, that is, unless it were caught in the act.

Sitting in his apartment, drinking a glass of milk, Mr. Martin reviewed his case against Mrs. Ulgine Barrows, as he had every night for seven nights. He began at the beginning. Her quacking voice and braying laugh had first profaned the halls of F & S on March 7, 1941 (Mr. Martin had a head for dates). Old Roberts, the personnel chief, had introduced her as the newly appointed special adviser to the president of the firm, Mr. Fitweiler. The woman had appalled Mr. Martin instantly, but he hadn't shown it. He had given her his dry hand, a look of studious concentration, and a faint smile. "Well," she had said, looking at the papers on his desk, "are you lifting the oxcart out of the ditch?" As Mr. Martin recalled that moment, over his milk, he squirmed slightly. He must keep his mind on her crimes as a special adviser, not on her peccadillos as a personality. This he found difficult to do, in spite of entering an objection and sustaining it. The faults of the woman as a woman kept chattering on in his mind like an unruly witness. She had, for almost two years now, baited him. In the halls, in the elevator, even in his own office, into which she romped now and then like a circus horse, she was constantly shouting these silly questions at him. "Are you lifting the oxcart out of the ditch? Are you tearing up the pea patch? Are you hollering down the rain barrel? Are you scraping around the bottom of the pickle barrel? Are you sitting in the catbird seat?"

It was Joey Hart, one of Mr. Martin's two assistants, who had explained what the gibberish meant. "She must be a Dodger fan," he had said. "Red Barber announces the Dodger games over the radio and he uses those expressions—picked 'em up down South." Joey had gone on to explain one or two. "Tearing up the pea patch" meant going on a rampage; "sitting in the catbird seat" meant sitting pretty, like a batter with three balls and no strikes on him. Mr. Martin dismissed all this with an effort. It had been annoying, it had driven him near to distraction, but he was too solid a man to be moved to murder by anything so childish. It was fortunate, he reflected as he passed on to the important charges against Mrs. Barrows, that he had stood up under it so well. He had maintained always an outward appearance of polite tolerance. "Why, I even believe you like the woman," Miss Paird, his other assistant, had once said to him. He had simply smiled.

A gavel rapped in Mr. Martin's mind and the case proper was resumed. Mrs. Ulgine Barrows stood charged with willful, blatant, and persistent attempts to destroy the efficiency and system of F & S. It was competent, material, and relevant to review her advent and rise to power. Mr. Martin had got the story from Miss Paird, who seemed always able to find things out. According to her, Mrs. Barrows had met Mr. Fitweiler at a party, where she had rescued him from the embraces of a powerfully built drunken man who had mistaken the president of F & S for a famous retired Middle Western football coach. She had led him to a sofa and somehow worked upon a monstrous magic. The aging gentleman had jumped to the conclusion there and then that this was a woman of singular attainments, equipped to bring out the best in him and in the firm. A week later he had introduced her into F & S as his special adviser. On that day confusion got its foot in the door. After Miss Tyson, Mr. Brundage, and Mr. Bartlett had been fired and Mr. Munson had taken his hat and stalked out, mailing in his resignation later, old Roberts had been emboldened to speak to Mr. Fitweiler. He mentioned that Mr. Munson's department had been "a little disrupted" and hadn't they perhaps better resume the old system there? Mr. Fitweiler had said certainly not. He had the greatest faith in Mrs. Barrow's ideas. "They require a little seasoning, a little seasoning, is all," he had added. Mr. Roberts had given it up. Mr. Martin reviewed in detail all the changes wrought by Mrs. Barrows. She had begun chipping at the cornices of the firm's edifice and now she was swinging at the foundation stones with a pickaxe.

Mr. Martin came now, in his summing up, to the afternoon of Monday, November 2, 1942—just one week ago. On that day, at 3 P.M., Mrs. Barrows had bounced into his office. "Boo!" she had yelled. "Are you scraping around the bottom of the pickle barrel?" Mr. Martin had looked at her from under his green eyeshade, saying nothing. She had begun to wander about the office, taking it in with her great, popping eyes. "Do you really need *all* these filing cabinets?" she had demanded suddenly. Mr. Martin's heart had jumped. "Each of these files," he had said, keeping his voice even, "plays an indispensable part in the system of F & S." She had brayed at him, "Well, don't tear up the pea patch!" and gone to the door. From there she had bawled, "But you sure have got a lot of fine scrap in here!" Mr. Martin could no longer doubt that the finger was on his beloved department. Her pickaxe was on the upswing, poised for the first blow. It had not come yet; he had received no blue memo from the enchanted Mr. Fitweiler bearing nonsensical instructions deriving from the obscene woman. But there was no doubt in Mr. Martin's mind that one would be forthcoming. He must act quickly. Already a precious week had gone by. Mr. Martin stood up in his living room, still holding his milk glass. "Gentlemen of the jury," he said to himself, "I demand the death penalty for this horrible person."

The next day Mr. Martin followed his routine, as usual. He polished his glasses more often and once sharpened an already sharp pencil, but not even Miss Paird noticed. Only once did he catch sight of his victim; she swept past him in the hall with a patronizing "Hi!" At five-thirty he walked home, as usual, and had a glass of milk, as usual. He had never drunk anything stronger in his life—unless you could count ginger ale. The late Sam Schlosser, the S of F & S, had praised Mr. Martin at a staff meeting several years before for his temperate habits. "Our most efficient worker neither drinks nor smokes," he had said. "The results speak for themselves." Mr. Fitweiler had sat by, nodding approval.

Mr. Martin was still thinking about that red-letter day as he walked over to the Schrafft's on Fifth Avenue near Forty-sixth Street. He got there, as he always did, at eight o'clock. He finished his dinner and the financial page of the *Sun* at a quarter to nine, as he always did. It was his custom after dinner to take a walk. This time he walked down Fifth Avenue at a casual pace. His gloved hands felt moist and warm, his forehead cold. He transferred the Camels from his overcoat to a jacket pocket. He wondered, as he did so, if they did not represent an unnecessary note of strain. Mrs. Barrows smoked only Luckies. It was his idea to puff a few puffs on a Camel (after the rubbing-out), stub it out in the ashtray holding her lipstick-stained Luckies, and thus drag a small red herring across the trail. Perhaps it was not a good idea. It would take time. He might even choke, too loudly.

Mr. Martin had never seen the house on West Twelfth Street where Mrs. Barrows lived, but he had a clear enough picture of it. Fortunately, she had bragged to everybody about her ducky first-floor apartment in the perfectly darling three-story red-brick. There would be no doorman or other attendants; just the tenants of the second and third floors. As he walked along, Mr. Martin realized that he would get there before nine-thirty. He had considered walking north on Fifth Avenue from Schrafft's to a point from which it would take him until ten o'clock to reach the house. At that hour people were less likely to be coming in or going out. But the procedure would have made an awkward loop in the straight thread of his casualness, and he had abandoned it. It was impossible to figure when people would be entering or leaving the house, anyway. There was a great risk at any hour. If he ran into anybody, he would simply have to place the rubbing-out of Ulgine Barrows in the inactive file forever. The same thing would hold true if there were someone in her apartment. In that case he would just say that he had been passing by, recognized her charming house and thought to drop in.

It was eighteen minutes after nine when Mr. Martin turned into Twelfth Street. A man passed him, and a man and a woman talking. There was no one within fifty paces when he came to the house, halfway down the block. He was up the steps and in the small vestibule in no time, pressing the bell under the card that said "Mrs. Ulgine Barrows." When the clicking in the lock started, he jumped forward against the door. He got inside fast, closing the door behind him. A bulb in a lantern hung from the hall ceiling on a chain seemed to give a monstrously bright light. There was nobody on the stair, which went up ahead of him along the left wall. A door opened down the hall in the wall on the right. He went toward it swiftly, on tiptoe.

"Well, for God's sake, look who's here!" bawled Mrs. Barrows, and her braying laugh rang out like the report of a shotgun. He rushed past her like a football tackle, bumping her. "Hey, quit shoving!" she said, closing the door behind them. They were in her living room, which seemed to Mr. Martin to be lighted by a hundred lamps. "What's after you?" she said. "You're as jumpy as a goat." He found he was unable to speak. His heart was wheezing in his throat. "I—yes," he finally brought out. She was jabbering and laughing as she started to help him off with his coat. "No, no," he said. "I'll put it here." He took it off and put it on a chair near the door. "Your hat and gloves, too," she said. "You're in a lady's house." He put his hat on top of the coat. Mrs. Barrows seemed larger than he had thought. He kept his gloves on. "I was passing by," he said. "I recognized—is there anyone here?" She laughed louder than ever. "No," she said, "we're all alone. You're as white as a sheet, you funny man. Whatever has come over you? I'll mix you a toddy." She started toward a door across the room. "Scotch-and-soda be all right? But say, you don't drink, do you?" She turned and gave him her amused look. Mr. Martin pulled himself together. "Scotch-and-soda will be all right," he heard himself say. He could hear her laughing in the kitchen.

Mr. Martin looked quickly around the living room for the weapon. He had counted on finding one there. There were andirons and a poker and something in a corner that looked like an Indian club. None of them would do. It couldn't be that way. He began to pace around. He came to a desk.

On it lay a metal paper knife with an ornate handle. Would it be sharp enough? He reached for it and knocked over a small brass jar. Stamps spilled out of it and it fell to the floor with a clatter. "Hey," Mrs. Barrows yelled from the kitchen, "are you tearing up the pea patch?" Mr. Martin gave a strange laugh. Picking up the knife, he tried its point against his left wrist. It was blunt. It wouldn't do.

When Mrs. Barrows reappeared, carrying two highballs, Mr. Martin, standing there with his gloves on, became acutely conscious of the fantasy he had wrought. Cigarettes in his pocket, a drink prepared for him—it was all too grossly improbable. It was more than that; it was impossible. Somewhere in the back of his mind a vague idea stirred, sprouted. "For heaven's sake, take off those gloves," said Mrs. Barrows. "I always wear them in the house," said Mr. Martin. The idea began to bloom, strange and wonderful. She put the glasses on a coffee table in front of a sofa and sat on the sofa. "Come over here, you odd little man," she said. Mr. Martin went over and sat beside her. It was difficult getting a cigarette out of the pack of Camels, but he managed it. She held a match for him, laughing. "Well," she said, handing him his drink, "this is perfectly marvelous. You with a drink and a cigarette."

Mr. Martin puffed, not too awkwardly, and took a gulp of the highball. "I drink and smoke all the time," he said. He clinked his glass against hers. "Here's nuts to that old windbag, Fitweiler," he said, and gulped again. The stuff tasted awful, but he made no grimace. "Really, Mr. Martin," she said, her voice and posture changing, "you are insulting our employer." Mrs. Barrows was now all special adviser to the president. "I am preparing a bomb," said Mr.

Martin, "which will blow the old goat higher than hell." He had only had a little of the drink, which was not strong. It couldn't be that. "Do you take dope or something?" Mrs. Barrows asked coldly. "Heroin," said Mr. Martin. "I'll be coked to the gills when I bump that old buzzard off." "Mr. Martin!" she shouted, getting to her feet. "That will be all of that. You must go at once." Mr. Martin took another swallow of his drink. He tapped his cigarette out in the ashtray and put the pack of Camels on the coffee table. Then he got up. She stood glaring at him. He walked over and put on his hat and coat. "Not a word about this," he said, and laid an index finger against his lips. All Mrs. Barrows could bring out was "Really!" Mr. Martin put his hand on the doorknob. "I'm sitting in the catbird seat," he said. He stuck his tongue out at her and left. Nobody saw him go.

Mr. Martin got to his apartment, walking, well before eleven. No one saw him go in. He had two glasses of milk after brushing his teeth, and he felt elated. It wasn't tipsiness, because he hadn't been tipsy. Anyway, the walk had worn off all effects of the whisky. He got in bed and read a magazine for a while. He was asleep before midnight.

Mr. Martin got to the office at eight-thirty the next morning, as usual. At a quarter to nine, Ulgine Barrows, who had never before arrived at work before ten, swept into his office. "I'm reporting to Mr. Fitweiler now!" she shouted. "If he turns you over to the police, it's no more than you deserve!" Mr. Martin gave her a look of shocked surprise. "I beg your pardon?" he said. Mrs. Barrows snorted and bounced out of the room, leaving Miss Paird and Joey Hart staring after her. "What's the matter with that old devil now?" asked Miss Paird. "I have no idea," said Mr. Martin, resuming his work. The other two looked at him and then at each other. Miss Paird got up and went out. She walked slowly past the closed door of Mr. Fitweiler's office. Mrs. Barrows was yelling inside, but she was not braying. Miss Paird could not hear what the woman was saying. She went back to her desk.

Forty-five minutes later, Mrs. Barrows left the president's office and went into her own, shutting the door. It wasn't until half an hour later that Mr. Fitweiler sent for Mr. Martin. The head of the filing department, neat, quiet, attentive, stood in front of the old man's desk. Mr. Fitweiler was pale and nervous. He took his glasses off and twiddled them. He made a small, bruffing sound in his throat. "Martin," he said, "you have been with us more than twenty years." "Twenty-two, sir," said Mr. Martin. "In that time," pursued the president, "your work and your—uh—manner have been exemplary." "I trust so, sir," said Mr. Martin. "I have understood, Martin," said Mr. Fitweiler, "that you have never taken a drink or smoked." "That is correct, sir," said Mr. Martin. "Ah, yes." Mr. Fitweiler polished his glasses. "You may describe what you did after leaving the office yesterday, Martin," he said. Mr. Martin allowed less than a second for his bewildered pause. "Certainly, sir," he said. "I walked home. Then I went to Schrafft's for dinner. Afterward I walked home again. I went to bed early, sir, and read a magazine for a while. I was asleep before eleven." "Ah, yes," said Mr. Fitweiler again. He was silent for a moment, searching for the proper words to say to the head of the filing department. "Mrs. Barrows," he said finally, "Mrs. Barrows has worked hard, Martin, very hard. It grieves me to report that she has suffered a severe breakdown. It has taken the form of a persecution complex accompanied by distressing hallucinations." "I am very sorry, sir," said Mr. Martin. "Mrs. Barrows is under the delusion," continued Mr. Fitweiler, "that you visited her last evening and behaved yourself in an—uh—unseemly manner." He raised his hand to silence Mr. Martin's little pained outcry. "It is the nature of these psychological diseases," Mr. Fitweiler said, "to fix upon the least likely and most innocent party as the—uh—source of persecution. These matters are not for the lay mind to grasp, Martin. I've just had my psychiatrist, Dr. Fitch, on the phone. He would not, of course, commit himself, but he made enough generalizations to substantiate my suspicions. I suggested to Mrs. Barrows when she had completed her—uh—story to me this morning, that she visit Dr. Fitch, for I suspected a condition at once. She flew, I regret to say, into a rage, and demanded—uh—requested that I call you on the carpet. You may not know, Martin, but Mrs. Barrows had planned a reorganization of your department—subject to my approval, of course, subject to my approval. This brought you, rather than anyone else, to her mind—but again that is a phenomenon for Dr. Fitch and not for us. So, Martin, I am afraid Mrs. Barrows' usefulness here is at an end." "I am dreadfully sorry, sir," said Mr. Martin.

It was at this point that the door to the office blew open with the suddenness of a gas-main explosion and Mrs. Barrows catapulted through it. "Is the little rat denying it?" she screamed. "He can't get away with that!" Mr. Martin got up and moved discreetly to a point beside Mr. Fitweiler's chair. "You drank and smoked at my apartment," she bawled at Mr. Martin, "and you know it! You called Mr. Fitweiler an old windbag and said you were going to blow him up when you got coked to the gills on your heroin!" She stopped yelling to catch her breath and a new glint came into her popping eyes. "If you weren't such a drab, ordinary little man," she said, "I'd think you'd planned it all. Sticking your tongue out at me, saying you were sitting in the catbird seat, because you thought no one would believe me when I told it! My God, it's really too perfect!" She brayed loudly and hysterically, and the fury was on her again. She glared at Mr. Fitweiler. "Can't you see how he has tricked us, you old fool? Can't you see his little game?" But Mr. Fitweiler had been surreptitiously pressing all the buttons under the top of his desk and employees of F & S began pouring into the room. "Stockton," said Mr. Fitweiler, "you and Fishbein will take Mrs. Barrows to her home. Mrs. Powell, you will go with them." Stockton, who had played a little football in high school, blocked Mrs. Barrows as she made for Mr. Martin. It took him and Fishbein together to force her out of the door into the hall, crowded with stenographers and office boys. She was still screaming imprecations at Mr. Martin, tangled and contradictory imprecations. The hubbub finally died out down the corridor.

"I regret that this has happened," said Mr. Fitweiler. "I shall ask you to dismiss it from your mind, Martin." "Yes, sir," said Mr. Martin, anticipating his chief's "That will be all" by moving to the door. "I will dismiss it." He went out and shut the door, and his step was light and quick in the hall. When he entered his department he had slowed down to his customary gait, and he walked quietly across the room to the W20 file, wearing a look of studious concentration.

# The Star-Spangled Banner

by Francis Scott Key

*It was 1814 and the United States had been waging war with the British for two years. Francis Scott Key, a Washington lawyer being held hostage aboard a British ship, watched in horror as the British attacked Fort McHenry. The incredible survival of Fort McHenry inspired Key to write "The Star-Spangled Banner."*

O say can you see by the dawn's early light
   What so proudly we hail'd at the
   twilight's last gleaming,
Whose broad stripes and bright stars
   through the perilous fight
O'er the ramparts we watch'd,
   were so gallantly streaming?
5   And the rockets' red glare,
   the bombs bursting in air,
Gave proof through the night
   that our flag was still there,
O say does that star-spangled banner yet
   wave
O'er the land of the free and the home of
   the brave?

On the shore dimly seen through the mists
   of the deep,
10   Where the foe's haughty host in dead
   silence reposes,

What is that which the breeze, o'er the
    towering steep,
As it fitfully blows, half conceals, half dis-
    closes?
Now it catches the gleam of the
    morning's first beam
In full glory reflected now shines
    in the stream
15  'Tis the star-spangled banner—O long may it
    wave
O'er the land of the free and the home of
    the brave!

And where is that band who so vauntingly
    swore,
That the havoc of war and the battle's
    confusion
A home and a Country should leave us no
    more?
20  Their blood has wash'd out their foul
    footstep's pollution.
No refuge could save their hireling and slave
From the terror of flight or the gloom of the
    grave,
And the star-spangled banner in triumph
    doth wave
O'er the land of the free and the home of
    the brave.

25  O thus be it ever when freemen shall stand
Between their lov'd home and the war's des-
    olation!
Blest with vict'ry and peace may the heav'n
    rescued land
Praise the power that hath made and
    preserv'd us a nation!

Then conquer we must, when our cause it is
    just,
30  And this be our motto—"In God We Trust,"
    And the star-spangled banner in triumph
        shall wave
    O'er the land of the free and the home of
        the brave.